# Let Me Out of My Mind

## Breaking Free from Mental Illness

### A Journey to the Light

J. Oliva

**DISCLAIMER:**

This is a true story based on the testimony and actual truthful accounts of one individual's life events. Results disclosed are not typical. All the material contained in this book is provided for educational and informational purposes only. All advice, guidance and recommendations contained herein should be taken at the sole discretion of the reader and shall, in no way, shape or form, replace the expert advice of a medical professional. Please do and adhere to whatever is best for your own personal situation. No responsibility against the author and/or publisher can be taken for any results or outcomes resulting from the use or misuse of this material.

Book cover illustration accredited to:
Dillumination © TMarchev | Dreamstime.com

CreateSpace Independent Publishing
ISBN-13: 978-1512201390
ISBN-10: 1512201391

# Table of Content

# DEDICATION

First and foremost, I want to thank God for guiding me to the light and giving me a second chance to live a beautiful, rewarding and abundant life full of love and good health.

I dedicate this book to both my children, Robert and Jaclyn. You have both been my rock and gave me the courage and inspiration I needed to overcome great obstacles. Thank you for *believing* in me when I didn't *believe* in myself. You two are the biggest blessing given to me by God.

To my beautiful and sweet mom. I deeply appreciate all the sacrifices that you made for me. I wish I could have helped you more by teaching you the valuable lessons I share in this book. I realize that your Alzheimer's prevents you from ever reading nor understanding any of this, but my hope is that our healthy souls will reconnect one day and that somewhere in your heart, you know how much I love you.

And to everyone who never understood me and supported me regardless. I thank you all for your unconditional love and for never giving up on me!

*In Loving Memory of*
*Armando Fidelio Oliva*
**R.I.P. Daddy**

# Prologue

As THE BLOOD SEEPS out of the self-inflicted wounds off my wrists, my thirteen year old son looks down with horror on his face. With pure heart break, he watches from a distance while the paramedics arrive and bandage my wrists. The terror penetrates his soul while he witnesses them placing me on a gurney as they hurry me away in an ambulance. He rushes back to his bed with this tainted vision and a flood of tears running down his face wondering, "What happened? What is wrong with my mom? Is she going to die? Why couldn't I help her?"

There was no doubt that I had fallen trap to the powers of a negative mind-set. The destructive consequence from a person's mental deficiency can be life-threatening if not better understood. Mental illness is a condition that many do not identify with, let alone is it understood by the sufferer and its' victims. How can we better understand and overcome this condition is my mission in this book?

Do you or does someone you know suffer from any type of mental illness? Have you found that depression alone has interfered with your daily life or your loved ones? Do you find yourself always struggling to help someone with a negative mind-set, or does your own negativity interfere with your daily productivity? Have you ever wished that you could change everything around you and make it all better?

It is understood that any condition that interferes with your thinking, changes in moods, your inability to relate to others that causes you social withdrawal is known as some sort of mental instability and/or impairment. When this condition becomes the center of your life, society perceives that you are experiencing a form of mental illness.

Mental illness is a stigmatized label where many different unstable emotional conditions are grouped together. Examples of these conditions commonly known by the general public are depression, bipolar disorder, schizophrenia, eating disorders and addictive personalities, to name just a few. One of the most controversial and less talked about is multiple personality disorder, also known now as dissociative identity disorder.

So, how can you be sure which condition you or your loved one suffers from and why? Can you suffer from more than one mental illness? There are more than 200 classified forms of mental illnesses, making it a very complex question to decipher. However, acceptance that there is a problem is the first step in getting to the root of this dilemma. Perhaps seeking out help from a professional is another step, which, unfortunately, most Americans refuse to take.

In my opinion, entering the self-discovery phase, which is *the process of acquiring insight into one's own character*, is probably the hardest step to accomplish.

Unfortunately, most Americans are afraid of the term mental illness; therefore, they refuse to acknowledge they have any type of impairment in order to avoid falling into a mental illness category.

What many fail to recognize is that regardless on the severity of their emotional deficiency, any state of mental impairment can be caused by environmental stresses and/or childhood conditioning, genetic factors, biochemical imbalances, or a combination of them all. Society lacks the understanding that it is not the individual's fault for possessing such a condition. This causes the afflicted individual to isolate themselves away from society, feeling alone with their struggles.

I have come to learn first-hand that society, in general, can become extremely cruel in terms of discrimination regarding the mental illness stigma. This is a big problem, as it causes most Americans, or anyone from any culture, to avoid disclosing their personal struggles to anyone, fearing some sort of alienation for making known that internal suffering exists. Emotional weakness is the most common accusation towards the afflicted.

Just like cancer, diabetes, and heart disease, mental illness carries its own detrimental death sentence if not properly treated, with suicide sometimes being the result. This stems from individuals becoming trapped in their minds. Their mind-set of helplessness and hopelessness produce a great deal of loneliness. Denial becomes their biggest enemy, as it is their only defense in preserving their dignity. One's own thought process becomes tarnished somehow, and without proper treatment and self-discovery, their mind will continue to foster damaging results. Awareness is the key in combating such a possible life-threatening condition.

Roughly 80 to 90 percent of individuals that seek treatment for depression receive lifesaving results. Disappointingly, approximately 15 percent who are clinically depressed consequently die by suicide. To its detriment, as reported by the Centers for Disease Control and Prevention (CDC), over 40,000 *Americans lost their lives by suicide in the year 2012* alone. It is estimated that *60 percent of all who die by suicide suffered from major depression.*

My father died on December 25, 2003 by suicide resulting from major depression. I personally have attempted suicide at least six to seven times during my lifetime. A further troubling experience for me was witnessing both my children endure some sort of depression during their adolescent and adulthood years.

In the year 2014, a very public and prominent figure died by suicide, Robin Williams. His death alone brought upon much public awareness on the subject, but I am noticing that this awareness is again fading fast. Most recently, I was made aware of another elderly male family friend who committed suicide.

Their demise, along with my father's, propelled me to finally pursue my journey in attempting to bring about more consciousness on the matter. My challenge is to help others break-free from mental illness as I have been able to do.

I was once too afraid to reveal my story, all due to my "fear" of the general public's ignorance and insensitivity toward the matter. Why would anyone care what I have to say anyway, right?

Regardless of what anyone thinks, I chose not to be afraid anymore!

After my father passed away, I attended a grieving counseling group for individuals who had also lost their loved ones by suicide. Two of the biggest questions I came across were, "How could they have done such a thing? Didn't they think of what it would do to those that loved them?"

I was also presented with these same questions from my own family members regarding my father's suicide. I found myself being able to relate to my father's and others' frame of mind during their final moments and only because I had found myself there too, moments before my suicide attempts. I understood the utter frustration of being trapped in an irrational way of thinking where one feels that the only way out is death.

Although I attempted to give others some insight on how a trapped and irrational mind thinks, it was impossible for me to really help them understand at the time, simply because I was still a sufferer. I was still struggling in how to escape the battle within my own mind that was robbing me of leading a healthy and productive life. Even though I understood how it felt during those illogical moments, I didn't know how to break-free from it.

My father's suicide, as devastating as it was, actually helped me venture out on a journey to figure out why I was plagued with mental illness by undergoing the self-discovery process. My father's death helped me to finally understand the pain it leaves behind for suicide victims' loved ones. This allowed me to see life from a different perspective.

I promised my children that I would never inflict upon them the pain my father left us all to bear. But, at the time, reality hit me, and I questioned, "How do I accomplish this if my mind is still so trapped?"

It wasn't until after fourteen years of intense psychotherapy and medication management with a forensic psychiatrist that I became stable enough to open up to new ideas for treatment.

Once my diagnoses were established through psychotherapy, overcoming these debilitating disorders I was beset with was the struggle of a lifetime. So the new ideas that were presented to me became my last resort to save my life and begin to live a rewarding life, unlike my father was able to do so, and to also give my children the loving and stable mother they longed for.

My quest in this book is to help you enter my extensively troubled mind as well as understand how it thought, reasoned, and processed information. I reveal how my suicidal mind worked. I will divulge how my journey of self-discovery brought about the mystery as to why my mind was so confined. When did it all begin?

The answers to my questions led me to a complete recovery that not even fourteen years of modern medical invention was able to accomplish.

Despite my biggest battle with mental illness, I also suffered with other ailments including fibromyalgia, gastritis, sinusitis, and pain from two herniated discs in my neck that required continuous spinal block injections. Once my mind was healed, all of these other ailments and pains seemed to, miraculously, slowly vanish as well.

Gradually, I learned that when the mind is not at ease, it can cause chemical imbalances that can subsequently cause all types of disease. Once the mind is at ease, it is *possible* to heal any disease one may have been stricken with.

Despite the fact that my conditions may be different than that of anyone else and my healing process is unique in its own way, I *believe* that anyone that battles with any mental deficiency, or any disease for that matter, can benefit somehow from my testimony.

As I take you through my healing journey, I will elaborate how my spirituality grew, resulting in an awakening I never fathomed was possible, where scientific findings along with faith-based *belief* has a remarkable correlation in healing the mind, body, and soul.

# Chapter 1:
# Dying to Die

FRANTICALLY, I LOCKED the bathroom door behind me. I took the hospital gown noose I'd secretly prepared and positioned it around the showerhead. I climbed on a chair and put the noose around my neck. I pushed the chair from under my feet. As my body hung there helplessly, all air supply was cut off in an instant. My face began throbbing with each beat of my heart. My eyes felt as if they were ready to pop out of their sockets. Suddenly, the noose slipped off the showerhead and the pressure was released. I was jolted and vigorously took a few deep breaths.

"Damn it," I thought to myself.

I rushed to do it again before anyone found me. I grabbed the noose and the chair and I climbed up to give it another try. Again, I put my neck around the noose and pushed the chair away from me. The weight of my body clamped my airways closed tightly. The pressure in my head immediately began to build again. My eyes were wide open, and I felt them bulging as if they were ready to burst. I hung there, very still, letting go of life. Darkness finally began to slowly creep in while my eye lids began to close. I began to enter what felt like a deep dark cold abyss. The more I entered into this suffocating world, the smaller and smaller the light became until it was completely out.

The next thing I remember was lying on the floor in excruciating pain. I could hear voices calling out my name saying, "Wake up, wake up."

I opened my eyes so ever slightly. I could see a glimpse of blurred light through the cracks of my eyes. My sight slowly began to focus, and I could see people's feet standing all around me. I was lying face down on the cold hard bathroom tiles with my head turned towards the right, dazed and without any memory of what had occurred. I felt pain coming from the left side of my head. I began to moan and moan. My eyes kept closing. The pain and confusion kept me puzzled with all that was happening around me. I could hear people talking frantically. It sounded like total chaos.

They cautiously turned me over on my back. I could see a bright light shine in my eyes while someone's fingers held them open. They put a hard brace around my neck and I could hear the wrenching sound of scissors hacking through my t-shirt and sweatpants. I was able to feel them remove the clothes from my motionless body and their hands touching every bone of every limb.

"Nothing appears broken," I heard someone say.

They kept asking me, "What happened? Why did you do this?" I could not seem to articulate a word. I just kept sighing as I closed my eyes, moving my head so ever slightly from side to side.

I again opened my eyes with a distressed look on my face, not understanding why they had stripped my clothes off, and then I saw them slip a hospital gown through my arms after which they covered me with a white bed sheet. They carefully placed me on a hard board and then, they lifted me onto a bed.

As I stared up at the ceiling, I could see the lights pass swiftly as they rushed me down the hall to another location.

"What just happened?" I internally wondered.

We finally arrived in a room with bright fluorescent lights, causing my eyes to squint. My lips began to shiver. It was so cold. I quickly recognized that I was in an emergency room. As I lay there baffled by all this pandemonium, my memory slowly returned.

My mind shockingly reflected, "It happened again! They are going to take me to the state hospital. I can't go back to the state hospital!"

When a nurse approached me, with an agonizing tone in my voice, I desperately asked, "Are they taking me back to State?"

I heard the nurse rush over and tell someone, "Tell the doctor she spoke. She is worried about going back to the state hospital."

I remember closing my eyes and recalling all of what had just happened, like a movie replaying in my head in slow motion: the noose, the showerhead, the pressure in my head, my eyeballs ready to pop out of their sockets. I now realized that the noose must have fallen again, but this time it left my unconscious body crashing down on the floor. The pain on the side of my head must have been my head slamming onto the hard floor tiles when I fell.

"Oh my God, what did I just do?" I was frightened.

I could not, however, remember why I was in the hospital in the first place. Nothing made sense other than the fact that I had lost all sense of time again and had one more unsuccessful suicide attempt under my belt. After several X-rays and a CAT scan, there were no signs of permanent damage to my head or body found, other than a big bump on my head.

I was hospitalized under a Baker Act order: a mandatory 72- hour involuntary hold in order to evaluate my mental health. Gratefully, I was told I would not be sent to the state hospital, as they decided to just transfer me into their own psychiatric unit despite the fact I had no health insurance.

It was then briefly explained that I was already at this hospital under a Baker Act order and was waiting to be transported to the state hospital. They found me after the state hospital had arrived to pick me up.

After they removed the brace from my neck and I was more alert, I looked down and noticed that both of my wrists were bandaged. I now remembered the reason I was in the hospital in the first place; I had slit my wrists for the second time. After the first attempt, I had been taken to the state hospital where I had an atrocious experience and swore I'd never go back.

Every time I awoke from such unexplained states of mind, it felt like I had been living in terrorizing nightmares. Why didn't I have control? Why? I just couldn't understand any of it.

I was thirty-three or maybe thirty-four years old; I cannot exactly remember. This was my sixth attempt to kill myself, or was it my seventh? I had been hospitalized so many times that is was hard to know for sure. I knew, though, that this appeared to be the worse attempt yet.

My distraught mental state seemed to be exacerbating. There was something locked up deep inside me that just wanted to die, and it would not stop until I succeeded. I was so afraid of myself, because there was that other part of me, however so slight, that wanted to stay alive. I still had a will to live, but I was petrified that one day that desire wouldn't be enough to combat that part of me that was dying to die.

# Chapter 2:
# A Secret War against the Demons Within

NOT BEING ABLE TO ESCAPE the hell that lived inside my mind was a torture beyond what any words can describe.

The absolute twisted world that consumed my every thought was more than I could bear. I simply had no clue why my mind lived in such a tormented existence. My need to understand how my mind worked and why I was suffering so much were all I cared about.

For most of my life, I felt blinded by pain and agony in what seemed to be a never-ending saga. I also questioned the whereabouts of that mystical spiritual entity who supposedly resides in the high-above heavens. Why, when I prayed, did my prayers seem to go unanswered? I had so many questions to ask, yet so few answers.

The only way to understand why I grew up with such distress, and how I got to the point where I felt the need to hang myself in a hospital bathroom, was to journey back to my past.

Taking this personal self-discovery venture was probably the hardest thing for me to do: to rehash everything in depth was extremely painful in its own recourse. Nonetheless, it was time to evaluate and put the pieces together of all the random memories that had surfaced during psychotherapy, hoping to decipher what happened to me. Why did I grow up in such mental confinement? When did it all begin?

"Surely I wasn't born this way?" I whispered in my mind.

"Is there a cure, or is it an illness that has me bound to eternal mental captivity?" I asked myself.

These were questions I had to evaluate closely. I desperately needed to undergo this self-discovery process in order to stop blaming others for my suffering and start taking responsibility for the life I was living and learn how to create the life that I wanted to live: free from such internal bewilderment.

Now I will continue to take you with me through my journey in figuring it all out. Why did I hang myself? What led me to that point?

My hope is that as we explore the mystery together, you will relate to my story somehow and allow yourself to reflect on your own personal voyage. My purpose is that this venture will help you to find the root cause for all the pain experienced so we can learn to dissolve the mental cause of it all.

As I revert back, the first sign of my deep internal distress was at the age of thirteen, which is when I ingested a bunch of pills I found around the house: Tylenol and tetracycline antibiotics. I wanted to escape the lonely world that I lived in. I wanted my mind to stop thinking. I just wanted to fall asleep forever. No more dreaming would be ideal.

As the pills churned in my stomach, it felt like a roaring volcano had exploded, spewing out hot acidic foam from my mouth. Afterwards, I cleaned up the mess and lay down in total despair.

"Why didn't it work?" I wondered, while strategizing on how to succeed the next time.

My relentless anguish propelled me to take the rest of the pills.

"This time it should work," I assured myself.

My mind grew drowsy, and again my stomach began to howl. It was time to make another attempt to reach the bodily fluid ejection station. As I stood up, my eyelids wanted to close, and my eyes rolled to the back of my head. I could not stand upright without holding onto something, but I stumbled to the proper expulsion room. I made it this time. As I knelt down and lowered my head, the volcano again erupted.

I slowly staggered back to my room, and my body seemed to get weaker and weaker. My limbs grew slack, and I fell to the ground in a heap, unable to move. The room was spinning as I lay there, recovering from the overwhelming amount of fluids I had just expelled.

Finally, my oldest brother found me. He immediately called my parents, and they rushed me to a nearby health clinic. The doctors were told that I simply had a bad headache and had taken too many pills. Neither of my parents could understand what was truly hidden within my troubled soul. The doctors chalked it up to just an unfortunate incident. They advised me of the dangers of taking too many pills and happily sent me on my way. Nothing really was done, and my family never spoke about this incident again.

In my desperate attempt to put the pieces of my childhood together, I wondered, "Why would anyone, let alone a thirteen-year-old child, be in so much mental distress that she would attempt to kill herself?"

I had to go back further and recall more, because there was more to unravel. There were too many pieces missing from this agonizing life-long journey.

After recalling a few more memories, it's possible that I'd begun to experience distressing moments at the tender age of twelve. I remember I didn't want to wake-up in the morning, and I did not want to go to school.

"But what makes that unusual? Don't all kids go through similar growing pains?" I pondered. "What made my situation so different to others?"

Well, as I continued deciphering my life, it was apparent that, for me, I was somehow feeling anxious to break-free from racing thoughts that consumed my mind. I anxiously wanted to stop thinking, never understanding why I felt this way.

Day after day, after completing my homework, I isolated myself in my bedroom with the lights out in pure darkness, laying there as I swayed back and forth in an attempt to somehow sooth myself. It was easy to turn-off the light switch, but there was no switch to turn-off my thoughts. I even played music in an attempt to divert my attention to anything other than the frantic thoughts that consumed my mind, but to no avail. It would take hours before sleep would arrive, to only experience nightmares of trying to run away barefooted on a long dark road. I'd sometimes wake-up huffing and puffing as if I had actually been running for hours. Finally, I'd drift back to sleep again. Then suddenly my mother was waking me up to go to school, exhausted as if I had not rested.

I kept my misery to myself.

Adding to my torment, every month I endured horrific painful menstrual cycles. It felt like my abdomen was swelling up like a balloon ready to burst. The pressure it inflicted on my lower back felt as if my hips were ready to break apart. The radiating pain would shoot down my buttocks into my thighs as it took over the entire lower part of my body. You could hear the agony in my voice as I cried out desperately for help. There were times when this torment would even include vomiting episodes.

My mother desperately tried to rescue me by giving me Tylenol, hot tea and placing hot compresses on my belly. She even resorted to wrapping my feet with hot towels. Nothing she did would calm down the intensity of those gruelling pains.

I could hear my father yelling in the distance saying how all I wanted was attention. He urged my mother to stop paying so much attention to me.

Ultimately I would be left all alone crying for hours: nobody to hold me, nobody to comfort me, and nobody to help me through my ordeal. This was a suffering I experienced month after month since the age of eleven. I dreaded that time of the month. Missing school a couple of days every month became part of my routine and another reason for my father to get angry at me.

I now recall there were many times that my father would hit me, sometimes slapping my face with his large thick hand busting my lip for things I never really understood. All I did know is that my mother and brothers all saw my father as a tyrant, and I was the only one who would speak-up and express my feelings against him. I always had a hard time with accepting abusive behavior and I made it known. I guess that was the reason I got my lip busted. How dare I speak against the house dictator, right?

I felt as if I just could never do anything right in his eyes. My brothers were always the good boys, and I was always the bad girl. At the very least, I surely wasn't the perfect little girl my father had always dreamed of.

I developed unrelenting resentment towards my father, because I perceived him as a mean and cruel man that never cared about my feelings, or anyone else's for that matter. My father's rough and abrasive behavior made me feel unloved by him. The utter frustration that was evolving inside me was like a bomb ready to detonate at any moment.

Again, as the nights approached, my thoughts would race— just like in those horrible dreams. I was trapped in a secluded world unknown to man.

As I attempted to forget any distressful moments in my life, I made every effort to continue living a normal life of an adolescent. We lived in a very small family community, and I would do my best to play with my best friend at her house as much as possible. We'd also ride our bikes and go visit other friends in the neighborhood. I'd do all I could to stay away from my house for as long as I could, because once I entered those doors, a sudden unhappiness seemed to creep in and take over.

There were so many disturbing angry encounters with my father, too many to mention, that always provoked me to hold in my anger despite my occasional verbal outbursts against him.

I now recall at age fifteen: due to my ongoing rebellious demeanor, my parents decided to take me to see a psychiatrist. All I knew during this time of my life was that I felt different from everyone else. Having to go see a psychiatrist just made me feel as if I were crazy. Nobody ever really explained anything about anything to me. I was just a troubled child who seriously needed help. I apparently had so much anger and rage locked up inside me that I didn't want to talk to anyone. I soon refused to see this doctor anymore, so my parents granted my wish, and I never saw him again.

By age sixteen, I had developed an extreme sense of self-doubt that threw me into a defiant state of mind. Skipping school became a ritual, because my inability to focus on my studies grew increasingly frustrating. Many times, I recall being with my friends and suddenly just passing out. I don't remember why, but I do know that they always called-out my name as I slowly snapped out of it.

One day I was taken to the school health clinic. It took four of my friends to pick me up off the ground: two holding my upper torso and two holding my legs, while a few others rushed in front of them clearing the way.

Upon regaining consciousness on a bed in the school clinic, I was told that my parents had been called. I later asked my friends to never do that again, because my father's reaction was more of a reprimand than of genuine concern. The rest of the school year is a complete blur.

Finally, my 9th grade year had ended and the summer was finally upon us. As the new school year approached, I received notification that I would have to repeat my ninth-grade year all over again. All my friends were moving on and I found myself overwhelmed with the news. I had never failed school before.

Whatever was happening in my mystified mind had obviously exacerbated to a point that it was now interfering with my academic work.

"What is happening to me?" I silently thought in despair.

I really could not imagine repeating a year that reminded me of such distress. Also, the thought of being in school watching my friends move-on was drastically upsetting to my already confused mind, so I took a bold stance and dropped out of high school; not caring how much it angered my father. There was nobody in the world that could make me get on that school bus and go to school.

Fortunately, with the help of a friend, I got a job in a clothing factory. Working somehow gave me a feeling of being all grown-up with a sense of accomplishment and independence, a feeling that failing school had taken away from me. In my mind, it was the only logical answer to my problems, regardless of how illogical that way of thinking may have been.

Despite my father's disapproval, he needed to keep me productive, so he sacrificed a great deal by driving me to and from work every day. He also agreed to enroll me in night school and then drove me back and forth to school each evening.

Being among other students that had also dropped out of high school helped me to feel as though I fitted in again. Realizing that I could probably obtain my high school diploma before my high school friends allowed me to build some confidence. I didn't feel I was failing anymore. I actually thought I was ahead of the game.

Yet this new journey did not last long. At age sixteen, one month before I turned seventeen, I got married to a nineteen-year-old man I had met at work only four months earlier, and I completely dropped out of school. His constant attention, flattering words, and sparkling interest won me over immediately.

Two weeks into dating, he asked me to marry him, and I said yes. He briefly spoke to my mom on the phone, and then he and his family came to meet mine.

At first my father was against it, but I assured him that if I had to run away and elope to another State that didn't require his approval, then that is what I was going to do.

I became a very strong willed young lady confronting my father every step of the way. I was going to get my way, no matter what it entailed. Ultimately my father gave in and agreed to walk me down the aisle.

The wedding plans had begun. Looking back now, I was obviously running away from something, and what it was didn't matter then, because I was sure that I had found unconditional love for the first time in my life.

I will never forget the day I was married, my father approached my husband and said, "She is your headache now." As much as that hurt me, I was also grateful that I would not live under his roof or dictatorship ever again.

After I was married, I got another job in an ice cream shop, located one block away from my new home. My new life had begun.

Continuing on this new path, one day before I turned twenty, I had my first child: a boy. Despite how happy I thought I was, my marriage slowly took a turn for the worse. As my husband and I began to grow up, we seemed to grow apart too. The yelling and screaming became our ongoing rhetoric. I obviously had a lot of hidden issues that would set me off at the drop of a dime. During my entire marriage, I felt as if I were living in an emotional roller coaster ride. The monthly menstrual cycles continued to haunt me as well. I even changed jobs more times than I can remember.

Although I kept learning a lot at each job, where I ultimately landed some impressive administrative assistant positions, I remained trapped in a very self-destructive mind-set, always blaming my husband for not growing up as quickly as I felt I was. I, obviously, developed an intense sense of denial regarding the turmoil that I possessed. I was secretly fighting a war against the demons that lived deep inside of my soul.

It wasn't until I found my three-year-old son hiding behind a chair in the living room, with his little hands over his ears, that I realized this destructive relationship had to stop.

Watching my son's reaction after witnessing all the intense arguing that surrounded him was like reliving my youth with my father. It gave me flashbacks of the times when I would curl-up like a ball in the corner of my bedroom during my father's raging episodes. I would rock back and forth moaning while digging the fingernails of my right hand into the back of my left—scratching and scratching until I eventually drew blood.

There was no way that I wanted my little boy to enter this frame of mind and resort to any type of destructive behavior as I had learned when I was young. So, at age twenty-three, I filed for divorce, ready to face my challenging life ahead as a single mom.

Being alone with my son, to me, meant nobody to fight with anymore: no more yelling and screaming. It was the only solution that made any sense at the time. Although my son was confused as to why his daddy had to leave, I thought, overall, he was adjusting to the situation quite well.

Despite my attempt to save my son from such distress, there was one night, shortly after his father and I separated and after putting him to bed, I heard a noise coming from the back door of our home. I immediately rushed to see what it was. I saw the back door open and when I looked out, I found my little boy outside walking around my car in the drive-way with a dazed look on his face. I rushed over and calmly brought him in the house and put him back to bed. I realized he was sleep-walking. He wasn't even four years old at the time.

This gave me further proof that what he had already witnessed along with my separation from his daddy had affected him far beyond what I had imagined. Part of me just began having thoughts of wanting to die again, because I was convinced that my personal distress had somehow damaged my son. I began to *believe* that my father was correct: I was a "headache" to all those who were near me.

It is obvious to me now, that controlling my thoughts of dying during troubling times was always hard, but gratefully during that time, I had an even deeper desire to help my child.

My profound concern with what was happening to my little boy helped me comfort him. I did my best to give my son as much love as I knew how during his waking moments: a love I never felt when I was his age. I also let him sleep with me in my bed. It appeared to help him a great deal. He seemed to be much more tranquil and never experienced a sleep walking episode like that again.

I was certain I had finally extinguished those horrifying thoughts and the yearning desire of wanting to die. My son was my inspiration to keep fighting through my internal mayhem and conquer those horrible feelings that I kept experiencing. I really thought that the secret war against the demons that once lived within me had vanished.

But was it really all over?

# Chapter 3:
# Desperate and Confused

DESPITE SOME VERY CHALLENGING and emotional times during the years that followed as a single mom, at the age of twenty-six, I experienced a very devastating moment in my life. I was raped on Christmas Eve by a man I had recently met and whom I entrusted to help me build a bike for my son. I wanted to place the bike under the Christmas tree to surprise him upon his return from his father's house on Christmas morning. Unfortunately, after the bike was built, the aggression began, turning it into a night of unthinkable horror.

After it was all over, the days that followed consisted of threatening phone calls by the perpetrator, assuring me that if I would tell anyone, he would come back and hurt my son.

I immediately confided in my ex-husband and requested he take my son until I found a new safe place to live. I was appreciative that his father and I had maintained an amicable and friendly relationship since our divorce. I immediately found an apartment and moved-out two weeks later on January 1st. Finally, my son was returned to me. I enrolled him in a new school and life went about making every attempt to put the past behind me.

As soon as I moved-out, I did my best to extinguish all memory of what had occurred by focusing on finally obtaining my high school diploma. This was a long-time goal I always wanted to achieve. So I bought a General Educational Development (GED) book, and relentlessly studied on my own, despite how difficult it was for me to focus. I had no time to think about anything other than studying. After a few months, I finally felt ready to take the exam.

I anxiously waited and waited for the results in the mail. A few weeks later, I opened my mailbox and I received the results. I was scared to open the envelope.

I swiftly walked back to my apartment, sat down and just stared at that envelope, deep in thought. I could feel my heart pounding; my hands were cold and clammy as they slightly trembled. I slowly opened the letter as I held my breath.

There it was, a few points shy of a passing grade, but I passed nonetheless. I was granted my high school diploma. I was so happy to have accomplished this goal all on my own. I released a big sigh of relief and I began jumping for joy in my living room.

"Yay, I did it, I did it," I kept shouting out with glee all by myself.

Regardless of this accomplishment, once there was nothing else to focus on, the memories of that horrific Christmas Eve began to surface once again. The dreams of running barefooted along a dark road, as I had when I was younger, had returned. These nightmares woke me up in cold sweats. The demons that once lived inside of me had once again returned.

"Why is this happening to me again? Why?" I was puzzled.

My inability to focus at work was becoming harder and harder as each day passed. This internal battle began to throw me into a dangerous downward spiral, like a plane that had lost its engines and was plummeting nose-first to the ground. I was going down fast.

I even sought-out help from a psychiatrist in my desperate attempt to avoid crashing to the ground. My session with him was so frustrating, feeling as if I were just spinning around in circles going nowhere. By the end of my session and during my drive home, all I could think about was how to run my car into a brick wall and simply end it all.

"What if I don't die instantly and I am awake to feel pain?" I contemplated.

The mere thought of experiencing pain from such an accident deterred me from following through with this plan. I just wanted to stop the pain, not to inflict even more of it.

This psychiatrist said I was experiencing depression and prescribed some medication. I didn't understand it all very well at the time, but if medication would help me lift-out of this fog I was in, then it was certainly worth a try.

So, I made an attempt to take the pills, only to get a stuffy nose. I now had a new problem. Breathing through my mouth caused excessive mouth dryness and I always felt as if I was suffocating. It would even make me wake-up several times at night. I didn't know what was worse, the so-called depression or the feeling of not being able to breathe properly. So, I stopped taking the medication and I never went back to see the psychiatrist again.

The next few months became more and more distressing. The flashbacks, the restless nightmares, the daily stressors of work while caring for my son alone began to catch-up with me. Also, those ruthless and unbearable monthly menstrual cycles that continued distressing me only exacerbated my internal battle.

Just like I'd miss school every month when I was a young girl; the same became a reality with my job. I was missing too much work. After a period of ten months, it was becoming too embarrassing to call in sick, as I was running out of excuses why I needed time off. It was all taking a toll on my life. My desperation and confusion grew worse.

There were nights when my son would have to tuck me into bed versus me doing it for him. This is how depressed I was. My inability to interact with my son as I had done in the past made me feel like a horrible mother.

Every morning I expected my little boy to get himself ready for school without my assistance, because mornings were difficult enough for me to get functioning, let alone to get him dressed and fed too. If my son didn't do as he should, I got angry and yelled at him all the way to school, saying that he had caused my rage. I told him that he could choose what kind of mommy I would be. If he did what he was supposed to do, I would be a good mommy, and if he didn't, I would become a bad one.

After dropping him off at school, I knew deep down that it was wrong to place this kind of responsibility on him. Still, I just couldn't seem to control my bursts of anger if things didn't run smoothly in the mornings. I hated myself for feeling the way I did, for behaving the way I did. The truth was that my behavior wasn't his fault. It was caused by the deep-rooted pain within me that kept surfacing. I just didn't know how to control myself. I really began to *believe* that my son would be better off without me in his life.

At age twenty-seven, I had made a couple more suicide attempts, just like when I was thirteen years old. With the first attempt, I went to the local drug store after dropping my son off at school and I bought a bunch of sleeping pills. I took them all and called my ex-boyfriend that worked for the same employer. I told him I was just too tired to go back to work anymore.

He knew all too well about my mood swings, so he immediately rushed over suspecting there was something wrong. I opened the door very drowsy. I told him I was very tired and that he had to leave. He boldly pushed the door open, walked in and started looking around while asking why I was so tired. He then found the sleeping pill box empty in the trash can.

Immediately after making this find, he picked me up and carried me to his car and took me to the hospital, despite my plea to leave me alone. I was too weak at that point to fight against his noble intensions. He also immediately called my parents. My mother met us at the hospital and my father made himself available to go pick up my son from school.

Upon arriving at the emergency room, I was immediately given some-sort of liquid charcoal to drink to detoxify my system, and I was placed under a Baker Act order and taken to their psychiatric unit. This was the first time I was ever in any place like this.

Once I snapped out of this irrational mind-set, I found myself in an environment with very unique and oddly behaving people I had never been around before.

"I don't belong here," I uttered to myself. "I must get out of here."

So I became very compliant with their strict rules and psychotherapy treatments. After the 72 hours elapsed, I was prescribed an antidepressant and sent home with further outpatient psychotherapy appointments.

Unfortunately, these new pills gave me very bad headaches that seemed to throw me into further despair. After a few weeks, the depression didn't seem to lift and the pounding in my head continued. So what did I do? I decided it was time to give this "falling asleep forever" idea another try. This time I took all the antidepressants I had left and downed it with a bottle of wine after, again, dropping my son off at school.

I called my father and asked if he could pick up my son after school because I wasn't feeling well. He agreed. I then proceeded to call-out from work again. Once my ex-boyfriend saw that I did not go to work, he came looking for me.

Yet this time it wasn't so easy for him to find me. I had strategically parked my car in another parking lot in my apartment complex and proceeded to walk back to my apartment. I barricaded my front door with my sofa. I calmly took my pills, drank my wine, made my phone calls and then went to bed.

"This time nobody will find me," I assured myself.

My ex-boyfriend got concerned when he did not see my car in my parking lot and anxiously went driving around looking for me. Fortunately for me, he found my car, but he got worried because I was not in it. He immediately called the police. He went back to my apartment and banged relentlessly on my door, but there was no answer. He decided to go look in my bedroom window and through the blinds he could see me lying on the bed. He banged on the window. I wasn't responding. The police had already arrived and called the paramedics.

They finally realized the window was unlocked. They opened the window and my ex jumped in. He rushed to open the door for the cops and paramedics and I was rushed to the hospital again.

That evening, I woke-up in the intensive care unit with a tube coming out of my mouth, and hooked up to all kinds of wires that were connected to my chest and arms. My parents and brother were standing at the foot of my bed.

As mother approached me, I will never forget the agonizing tone in my mother's voice when she asked me, "Why did you do this to me? Why?"

At that time, I could not empathize with her feelings. I was just baffled with the notion that I was still among the living.

This attempt came with a hefty penalty: a one-month hospitalization in the psychiatric unit. Curiously enough, though, at this facility I met an employee (a mental health counselor) who helped me through this difficult hospitalization period. We seemed to have built a very special bond, as I could not really engage in any reasonable conversation with anyone else. Our connection grew deeper and deeper resulting in us dating immediately after I was released.

It was very comforting to have him with me once I was home. Every time I experienced some sort of emotional distress, he would hold me like a baby in his arms to comfort me. This alone made me feel safe. Just to have someone understand me seemed like all I ever needed. A year later, at age twenty-eight, I married him.

Although I was diagnosed with clinical depression during this time, which required me to take medication, it is obvious to me now that I remained in denial and was reluctant to stay in treatment. (Clinical depression can result in the most severe form of depression, also known as major depression disorder.)

I was not too fond of taking medication, so I was noncompliant. Since my new husband was so supportive, I thought I had experienced only a temporary state of depression. I was certain that my depression was merely situational. I was just happy to finally have someone in my life that understood me for once and gave me the care and support I always needed. I convinced myself, back then, that with lots of love, understanding, and patience, I would be okay without medication.

By age twenty-nine, I had my second child: a girl. Yet this marriage became an extremely stressful and abusive relationship from the moment I got pregnant. My husband didn't want the baby and he wanted me to have an abortion. Although I tried to understand that he was undergoing a rigorous registered nurse program while working full time, and dealing with my emotional roller coaster ride was difficult for him, I just could not comply with his request.

Consequently, as soon as I made the decision to keep the baby, I just could not seem to do anything right in his eyes, no matter how hard I tried. I began to feel just like the time I lived with my father. The screaming, the arguing, and the disparaging name-calling gradually ate away any self-worth I had left.

Subsequently, I went into pre-term labor at 24 weeks, but my Obstetrician was able to hold off delivery until 36 weeks. In the interim, all the distress I endured caused five separate hospitalizations to keep the baby from being born early. Having to deal with such misery made this a pregnancy from hell.

"Where is the man who showed me so much love, understanding, patience, empathy, and compassion in the past?" I desperately questioned. "Why isn't he the same man anymore?"

I pleaded with God to help me understand, but the answer never came. Gratefully; however, my daughter was born very healthy.

Immediately after her birth, our fighting seemed to get worse. Once I was provoked, my sense of logic simply flew out the window. There were times when I felt as if I were losing my mind. I felt trapped in thoughts that nobody else could witness. I began to behave like a raging lunatic again, just as I had on those mornings when I took my son to school. I had no ability to reason.

Whenever I felt abused, it sent me off to a completely different world, a place where nobody else lived but me. As a result, I again was hospitalized in a mental health facility when my daughter was three months old. Their purpose was to get me back to a stable state of mind, but, unfortunately, I was still noncompliant with my medications. I simply despised the thought of taking medication.

Needless to say, the fighting continued, and I wanted out of this marriage. Breaking free from my mind seemed impossible and divorcing again appeared to be the only logical answer, but with two children, I didn't know how I could manage on my own.

I didn't want to keep my children in that abusive environment, where they would witness intense battles day in and day out. However, I didn't know how to get out of it either.

Fortunately for me, I was able to stabilize and acquired a respectable job when my daughter was six months old. It was with a very prominent organization. Somehow, this job gave me some kind of personal fulfillment that I had never received before.

Despite seeing my life experience some fulfilling purpose, the arguing in my marriage continued. As a result, I began to see my son at age twelve experience nightmares where he would wake-up in the middle of the night yelling and arguing as he would punch the wall by his bed. I remember rushing to his side to calm him, as he drifted back to sleep; never remembering the next day what he did the night prior. My son even began to sleep walk again, something he had not done since he was a little boy. My husband and I would booby-trap the front door by placing objects that would fall in hopes that it would make enough noise to wake us up. We feared he would just try to walk out during the middle of the night.

I began to witness the internal confusion that was, once again, building up in my sons mind. This alone distressed me a great deal. I worried about all the agony my son was experiencing as he continued to witness an abundance of disarray in the household.

At times, I even noticed how my son would take his little sister to another room to play and distract her when any heated argument flared up with my husband. It was my observation of his effort to protect her from witnessing any of our battles. Although I did all I could to help my son when he was younger by divorcing his father, the reality was that nobody else was ever there to help him when I couldn't. So despite his own personal confusion, he made every attempt to help his little sister.

I, again, started to feel helpless and trapped, not knowing what else I could do to help my children. I was thrown into an even deeper feeling of desperation than ever before. I didn't feel like I could protect my children any longer. I also began to suffocate from the strict daily obligations of wifehood my husband required as well. I felt more of a possession than a wife.

By age thirty-two, my deep-rooted mental anguish caused me to experience a severe nervous breakdown. On this one particular early morning before going to work, I remember my husband and I had engaged in a very heated argument. As I was getting ready for work, I kept trying to walk away from this combative atmosphere.

I felt as if I could not get away. I hurried to the bathroom, but he followed me. I hurried back to the bedroom, to the kitchen, but he was always there, spewing out hateful, disgusting words. I was finally able to finish putting on my make-up, got dressed and quickly walked out of the house. I got into my car hoping I could escape to work. I could feel my heart pounding as if it were ready to bust-out of my chest. My thoughts were racing so much that it felt like my brain was engorged. The stress was building so quickly that I was sure my mind was ready to explode. My hands were trembling as I attempted to put the key into the ignition. I don't remember anything else after that.

My son later explained to me that he and my husband both heard a blazing noise coming from the car, and they both took a dash to the front door. Once opened, they saw my lifeless body slumped over the steering wheel. My torso was causing the horn to blast, as if it were shouting out for help.

They ran to the car, opened the door and called out my name. They got no reaction from me.

Between the two, they sat me up and carefully pulled me out of the car. One grabbed my upper body and the other my legs as they carefully carried me back into the house. They continued to stagger all the way to the bedroom where they laid me on the bed.

I was oblivious of what had just occurred. My body was completely frozen: I could not move, speak, or react, just as I had in high school when my friends took me to the school clinic. Yet this time, I didn't snap out of it so easily. I was completely incapacitated for a few hours. Then, as I slowly returned to consciousness, my inability to communicate verbally lasted another three whole days until I eventually came back to reality.

I immediately sought-out professional help and began seeing a forensic psychiatrist. I was once again given the diagnosis of "clinical depression." It was explained to me that I had a chemical imbalance in the brain and had to take medication if I wanted my life to improve. Without a doubt, this was not situational depression. I finally realized that taking medication was mandatory at this point.

So I made a decision to comply with the treatment plan. I had to take a medical leave of absence from work, in order to recover and stabilize. One week after disclosing this information to my employer, I was fired. I literally felt as if my life was crumbling before my eyes: I was in an abusive marriage, I felt as if I were losing my mind, I could not care for my children, and I had lost my job. How much worse could life be?

After several psychotherapy sessions, my forensic psychiatrist became greatly concerned with my condition. He suspected there was more to consider than simply clinical depression.

With careful evaluation, he ultimately diagnosed me with the most controversial and misunderstood mental illness of them all, "multiple personality disorder" (MPD), which is also known as "dissociative identity disorder" (DID). This condition apparently stems from some type of serious abuse at a very early age—abuse I had locked up in my subconscious mind, abuse I had been able to reveal only to my psychiatrist.

This journey began when I was thirty-two, which led me to file for disability benefits. During the next two years, as I waited for a response from the government, the emotional and undisclosed abuse continued, and my condition consequently grew worse.

I was totally dependent on my husband's monetary support. I just didn't know how to escape his abuse, nor the chaos that lived within my mind and soul. My mind was severely trapped in a different world—a world inconceivable for any rational mind to understand.

Revealing my internal battle to my family was as if I were disclosing I was a failure in life, a failure my father always assured me I'd be, a failure I could not accept myself; so I never told a soul about this inner conflict.

*"Let me out of my mind!"* I pleaded God to help me, but with no benefit. I felt so confined, as the walls of the world slowly closed in on me. My irrational mind was convinced that death was the only way out of this torturous existence. During these years was when I slit my wrists and hung myself in the hospital. This is how severely desperate and confused I had become.

The question I had initially asked in the beginning of this self-discovery journey was answered. I finally understood what led me to hanging myself in the hospital. It was a series of events that trapped my subconscious mind, which all began at a very young age. These events created a great deal of clutter in my mind that eventually caused an excessive amount of internal pain that that my mind could not handle anymore. This pain began pouring out like a full glass of water that overflows with each drop that falls into it.

Regardless of this epiphany, as I continued on my self-discovery process, I questioned this new diagnosis given to me called Multiple Personality Disorder. I relentlessly asked, "How can different people live inside of me, claiming they are different ages with different names? How can that be, if they are all me?"

I remained both desperate and confused.

# Chapter 4:
# The Personalities

SOMETIMES I WAS CYNTHIA, age five—an innocent little girl who sucked her thumb as she curled up in a ball during my therapy sessions. Apparently, she had memories of how much I hated it every time my father stuck his hands down my panties and proclaimed my privates to be owned by him. Perhaps his intent was not sexual (or so I choose to *believe* to this day), but somehow, it was a feeling that made me extremely uncomfortable, a feeling I obviously wanted to forget.

Cynthia also expressed how she feared her father, because in her eyes, he appeared to be a cruel and heartless man who yelled all the time. She remembered how he once took her security blanket and shredded it into pieces during one of his angry states. She even held the memory of lying on her father's lap as he shoved something up her anus. She screamed for her mom to help her, not understanding that it was only a suppository to help bring down her fever, as I later learned as an adult from my mother. Yet the forceful way he did it was, without a doubt, a memory I also longed to forget.

These uncomfortable feelings somehow created Cynthia, because she was the one who harbored those awful memories that didn't surface until much later in life. I was just a little girl who wanted to play with my brothers, and I guess my subconscious mind created Cynthia so that I could go on with life as a normal little girl.

I can now recall behaviors I experienced during my younger years that may have attributed to the creation of Cynthia.

I remember how I used to get a lot of stomach aches and made strange complaints of always feeling sick. Missing school became a continuous ritual, because all I wanted was to stay home with my mom, who was home during the day and worked at night. I seemed to always seek-out comfort from my mother.

As a result, my parents would seek out medical assistance, yet they never found anything wrong with me. Ever since that very early age, my father began saying that all I wanted was attention—a claim he continued to repeat for years every time I made any kind of complaint.

It is obvious to me now that the internal pain hidden within my young mind had manifested in imaginary physical pains, because I just didn't know how to express it in any other way. As a result, when I was actually experiencing "real" pains, like with my menstrual cycle, nobody believed me. I was apparently viewed like the little boy who cried wolf. Not even was I able to detect fact from fiction. All I knew is that when I said I felt pain, it was certainly real.

Then there was Elizabeth, age twelve—another innocent young girl who claimed to protect Cynthia from being afraid all of the time. Elizabeth had a very sweet personality and displayed a great deal of strength by wanting to shield the little girl who lived within us. Her need was to be a protector, hidden behind a persona that nobody else knew existed, not even me. Elizabeth was somehow created to keep Cynthia calm whenever she felt afraid.

Another personality was Jenny O, age sixteen, a rebellious young lady who was apparently created to deal with the anger that stemmed from all of the things I had experienced during my younger years. Not only was there intense pain that threw me into attempting suicide at age thirteen, but there was additional sorrow I carried within me at age fourteen when I was robbed of my innocence by a twenty-year-old man. Although my virginity wasn't taken, every other sexual act was introduced to me including anal penetration. Somehow, I had a profound subconscious need to give away my father's possession to another man. Or perhaps I assumed that giving my private parts away was a way of showing love. I am not quite sure of my actual reasoning, but it was an unhealthy behavior, nonetheless. This caused me to accept statutory rape as being okay, as I was not aware, at that time, what happened to me was a criminal offense.

Consequently, due to the guilty feeling I endured, I *believed* that it was my fault for allowing it to happen. I just felt dirty and bad, and I apparently locked this memory away in another part of my subconscious mind because the shame became more than my conscious mind could bear. It was just too painful to carry around with me every day.

Then at age fifteen, I met a young man I truly had genuine feelings for and I gave up my virginity to him, trusting it was okay to do so. I had convinced myself that if I gave it to him, he would love me. But when that relationship didn't work out, I must have stored up this new pain in another section in my subconscious mind, making every attempt to forget all of the inappropriate things I had permitted.

This was during the time that my parents noticed my rebellious behavior exacerbate and attempted to seek out help by taking me to see that therapist who I refused to talk to.

By the age of sixteen, Jenny O accepted all of that pain that had been locked up inside my subconscious mind. The feeling of pure rebellion toward everything that had happened caused her to act out in every conceivable way, such as skipping school.

Perhaps the black-outs I experienced in ninth grade were a result of the creation of Jenny O, but who knows for sure? It is only speculation based on the series of events that surfaced in therapy.

One thing we do know is that Jenny O always displayed a bold and angry persona whenever she spoke during her therapy sessions. She was prone to uncontrollable angry outbursts throughout my life. She is the one who always said she wanted to die, simply to extinguish all of the pain that was locked up inside me.

Then there was Katherine, age twenty-seven, who spoke only once in therapy and never spoke to anyone else. It was also revealed that she protected the conscious mind from the devastating pain related to the rape that occurred on Christmas Eve, one month before I turned twenty-seven, because shutting down was the only thing she knew how to do during that traumatic experience. She is the one who learned to protect the self during very stressful and painful moments thereafter.

This revelation of Katherine's personality became evident when she relived this rape in one of her sessions with our MPD/DID specialized psychologist. This session was so intense that the psychologist was afraid that his colleagues would think it was him hurting me and not actually realize that it was me reliving that time in my life. Once the session was over, Katherine had moved from the couch to curl up in a ball behind a chair, as she cried profusely and revealed her name and age to our doctor.

When I awoke from this state of consciousness, I had no clue what had transpired until my doctor explained it all to me. Time seemed to have simply stopped, as losing time was such a scary experience. Waking up on the floor with my face drenched with tears is surreal to even remember. It was suspected that Katherine was the one who would lock me up in my mind, perhaps like when I was found slumped over the steering wheel.

Then there was Annabel, known only as the "Old Wise Woman." Ironically, Annabel first revealed herself to my ten-year-old daughter.

As I became more aware of my personalities and learned more about them, I discussed them with my children, so that they, too, could better understand what was happening to their mommy.

Although I had not revealed all of the abuse to them, I did try to educate them about multiple personality disorder and the actual names and ages of the personalities as well. I did the best I could to explain it to them, as I learned to understand it myself. I even reached a point where I had more control in allowing these personalities to surface on request by my doctors. It was the weirdest thing, but somehow it was now possible.

One day my daughter asked to speak with Cynthia; she wanted to meet the little five-year-old I had told her about. So, I dared to do what my doctors had helped me to do in their controlled and safe environment, where I'd learned to sit there quietly and somehow allow the transformation to take place in front of them.

My daughter explained to me, after I reverted back to being me, that I closed my eyes and then my eyes flickered up and down as my head also made small circular motions while I slowly transformed. I then somehow allowed Cynthia to come out.

My daughter said that Cynthia was just like a little girl who sucked her thumb and appeared frightened. At some point, there was a natural transformation where my daughter spoke to Elizabeth and then Annabel revealed herself as an "Old Wise Woman."

This personality had never surfaced before with my doctors. My daughter apparently asked her how old she was, and Annabel replied, "You never ask an old woman her age." My daughter seemed to get a kick out of that response, as she innocently giggled as she told me about her experience. I chuckled in laughter with her in order to down play what had just occurred.

I obviously did not recall their conversations, because I only know what my daughter told me. So it was suspected that Annabel became the wise one throughout the years, doing her best to hold everyone else together because she was obviously another protector. Annabel was apparently also a caregiver for my children when my mind was unable to do so. It's funny to think about it now, but my grandmother's name was Ana.

The mind has a mysterious way of working, doesn't it?

# Chapter 5:
# Confusing Life Changes

FINALLY, TWO YEARS AFTER filing for disability benefits, my request was granted by the government at age thirty-four. I was fortunate to have received two full years of retroactive disability income, and not only did I receive support for myself, but I received additional support for my children as well. Remarkably, a small light emerged at the end of this dark tunnel. With the retroactive government funds I received, I could put money down on a small foreclosed home and I filed for divorce. I was finally able to escape that abusive atmosphere.

In order to retain custody of our daughter, I assured my husband that I would not sleep until everyone knew the truth about all the disgusting, intense and appalling abusive details that he did to me. If I had to stand on the tallest mountain and "Tell, Tell, Tell," then that's what I would do in a court of law! So, if he wanted the divorce to go smoothly and quietly, he had to agree our daughter would reside with me despite how mentally ill I was. He ultimately agreed to let me have our daughter in order to protect his reputation and career.

The glorious day came and I finally moved out. I took only my children's bedroom furniture and our clothes. I left behind everything else we had acquired during the marriage, and I waived my rights to the home we had purchased together, as he agreed to waive his rights against the new home I had purchased. I just wanted to get out and get away. Material things didn't matter to me. Not only did I want to break away from this soul-destroying lifestyle, my goal was also to help my children live in an abuse-free environment. That was all I wanted to accomplish.

However, I will not lie, it was extremely difficult to live alone as a mentally ill single mom, raising both of my children, now aged fourteen and four. Living solely on the government's limited monthly funds and child support from my ex-husband was far from easy.

Although I was a nurturing mother, it was without a doubt a tremendously challenging time—not only for me, but for my children as well. All I knew was, despite all of the difficulties, this new home was our "safe place," and we were going to be okay. That alone was worth all of the sacrifices.

It was November 1996 when I was able to finally break-free from abuse entirely.

After my divorce was when I began to see the psychologist who specialized in MPD/DID. He was recommended by my forensic psychiatrist. During the preceding years, by maintaining consistency through both medication management and psychotherapy, a slight improvement was noticeable. It was during these years that all the details of the personalities really became clearer.

Then, in the year 2000, at age 38, I further improved after undergoing a full hysterectomy due to an extremely painful and debilitating condition I developed called endometriosis. (Endometriosis is an abnormal uterine condition where the tissues inside the uterus grow outside the uterus causing pelvic pain.)

Thereafter, not having my monthly cycles seemed to somehow lessen the frequency and intensity of my mental distress. I guess PMS (premenstrual syndrome) had also been a culprit in the exacerbation of my disability. In addition, being in an abuse-free household was of tremendous benefit to me.

As a result of this improvement, in 2003, at the age of forty-one, I completed a course in medical assisting and began to work part time, because I was still not mentally strong enough to work full time. I guess that my eagerness to become a productive member in society and my need to help others came from the agonizing road I had traveled along to get better myself. I seemed to have developed an overwhelming amount of empathy for the sick. I wanted to learn how to treat patients the way that many medical health professionals were unable to treat me.

You see, due to this mental illness, I encountered numerous non-empathetic healthcare workers. I felt as if a "mental illness" label was plastered across my forehead for all to see, although in reality, it was just plastered in my medical records.

I could probably write a separate book about all of the appalling encounters I endured during those years. It became obvious to me that although discrimination was illegal, it surely was evident. I experienced a very cruel world where any mental illness diagnosis was shunned upon. So, I wanted to make a difference not only in my life, but in the lives of others as well. Putting a smile on other people's faces during a time when they weren't feeling well was such a gratifying feeling.

Geriatric and mental health patients were always my favorite. They are the ones that always seemed to need the most empathy and compassion from me. They are the ones that appeared to appreciate that sort of attention the most, although all my patients expressed their overwhelming gratitude with the care I gave them. What a great sensation it is to make someone else feel good.

Unfortunately, by the end of 2003, on Christmas Day, I received the worst news: my father had committed suicide due to major depression. This alone set me back in my recovery process, and I lost my part-time job. I became a daily drinker in an attempt to extinguish the new pain that invaded my mind and soul. However, it wasn't until I landed in the hospital with an acute case of inflammation in the wall lining of my stomach (gastritis) that I was forced to curtail my drinking habit.

Regardless of how hard I worked to improve my mental health, at this time in my life, I was experiencing a lot of extreme "high" and "low" moments. My forensic psychiatrist became extremely concerned about these repeated mood swings.

I even remember telling a friend once, "I better get as much done as I can today, because tomorrow I might not be able to do anything." I was either going-going-going, or I was down and out for the count.

By the end of 2004, one year after my father's demise, and after some further evaluation, my psychiatrist suspected that I was also suffering from bipolar disorder. (Bipolar disorder is a mental disorder marked by alternating periods of elation and depression.)

This new diagnosis would have been a hard call to make in the past, because the monthly emotional roller coaster ride that followed my menstrual cycle and the uncontrolled multiplicity that was evident, meant the bipolar was difficult to detect. (Multiplicity is a state in which many people share one physical body.)

Now that the multiplicity was a little more under control and there was no longer a menstrual cycle, the bipolar became quite evident. So I was then prescribed a mood stabilizer, in conjunction with the pills I was already taking. It appeared to calm down my mood swings quite a bit.

By mid-2005, I made another attempt to further my education by taking a real estate course. I was encouraged to pursue this route because of a part-time job I had taken in a Realtor's office. Unfortunately, obtaining a part-time job in a medical office had become quite difficult as all I found were full-time positions. I was still not stable enough to acquire that type of full-time work. So back to the corporate world I went.

Three months after completing the Real Estate course, I got my real estate license and began working at my new career on a part-time basis. Unfortunately, I continued to battle with my mental distress and had many more psychologically challenging moments, but still, I didn't give-up. I had to always find some type of supplemental income, because living on disability and child support just wasn't enough to fully care for my children. I always kept striving to do better for them.

I did my best to work as much as I could during the times I would feel okay, but during those times that I wasn't, there was nothing I could do but recuperate. It was so tough, because I never had anyone to help me—nobody to knock on my door and say, "How can I help you?"

By mid-2007, my son was twenty-five years old and now working in the U.S. Coast Guard. He had struggled so much with my mental health condition that he made an attempt to help me by bringing me a book to read. Although he knew that my past reluctance to read books was due to my inability to focus well, he pleaded with me to read this one particular book.

"Mom," he said to me, "I know you don't like to read books, but this one is easy reading, and I really want you to read it. Please, Mom, read it. I know that you can do it."

He handed me a book called *The Secret*. I went to the beach, my favorite place on earth, for two days in a row one weekend, and I read the book in its entirety.

This was the first "Aha" moment I ever had, as Oprah Winfrey would put it. Something within my soul connected with each word, each sentence, and each paragraph. As I read, I remembered something I'd recently said to my psychiatrist. I'd asked him, "All of these years, I have learned that the mind is a very powerful thing; so much so, that my mind keeps controlling me. I just need to learn: how do I control my mind versus it controlling me?"

My psychiatrist replied, "I think you have reached a point where you will benefit from meditation. I can help you with this, if you'd like."

For whatever reason, I wasn't too receptive to the whole meditation thing, because I could not fathom how I could calm down my racing thoughts, so I never brought it up to him again.

Yet, as I continued to read *The Secret*, everything it said started to make sense.

"This is it," I realized. "This is the secret, but how do you do this? How can I manifest like this? How can I get better? I want to do learn how to do this." It was all I could think about.

Then I remembered that a friend of mine had recently told me about buying a movie called *The Secret*, but I'd never paid much attention to what she had said about it. I did remember that she mentioned purchasing the movie after being introduced to it on the *Oprah* show.

I called her and asked to watch the movie. In my personal opinion, the movie is much more powerful than the book. So I went out and bought the movie.

Although I watched the movie several times and did research on the Internet on how to connect with the Universe's energy and learn how to manifest, I seemed to fall back on my old conditioning, and I stopped watching the movie and doing my research altogether. As a result, my life continued on its dangerous emotional roller-coaster ride without any change.

I was reluctant to tell my psychiatrist about what I had learned, so we never discussed this during my therapy sessions. I was seeing him at this point mainly for medication management and to discuss daily coping skills. I seemed to keep falling into mini-crises that required his direct personal attention, so I never spoke to him about *The Secret*.

It wasn't until April 2008, when I was forty-six years old; that I decided I'd had enough of this crazy life. I really wanted my life to change, and I knew that if my life didn't transform, I would end up like my father: dead at the hands of my own killer . . . ME!

I also needed to find God!

"Where is this God everyone talks about?" I kept questioning. "Where is this miraculous Spiritual Entity who is supposed to make everything better, the one who is proclaimed to exist in the Universe?"

This is when I decided to use everything I had inside me to learn more about God, as I watched *The Secret* movie every single day. I simply could not stop watching the movie. I was fixated with it. *The Secret* was my daily reminder that this was possible somehow. It was the only thing that had ever made any sense to me.

During my intensive research on the internet, I also found an amazing mediation/manifestation audiotape that I downloaded for free, in hopes of learning how to quiet my mind and focus on what I wanted. I remembered what my psychiatrist had said to me about meditation and how it could help me, so I thought this would be good to try. I wanted to receive a healing so badly, and I incorporated this audio into my daily practice after watching the movie *The Secret*. This became my ritual, day after day, month after month. This became my personal secret, one I didn't disclose to anyone; not even to my psychiatrist.

All I knew was that I wanted to be healed and live a productive life in society. I wanted to stop depending on all of my medications: three types of meds, a total of seven pills a night (an antidepressant, a mood stabilizer, and an anti-anxiety pill). I wanted to learn how to control my mind versus it controlling me. I just wanted to be normal or, at least, what society perceived to be normal.

I desperately wanted to be happy. I wanted to feel as if I was worth something. I wanted to become a mother that my children could be proud of. I wanted to become the daughter and the sister my family yearned to have. What I mostly wanted was to stay alive and live a fulfilling life. I did not want to die like my father had. I wanted to break away from that deep dark pit I had been living in. I wanted to break out of those shackles that had imprisoned me all of my life! I wanted to escape the torturous existence that held me captive in my mind.

"Please, *let me out of my mind*," I inwardly continued my plea to God.

So in April 2008, I began a journey of putting *The Secret* to the test. I was out of options, and this was my last hope. It was pretty much do or die. Something deep down inside me *believed* that if I could master connecting with the Universe's proclaimed powers, I would be healed, just as the woman was healed from cancer in the movie *The Secret* and just like the man who was able to walk again after enduring paralysis from a plane accident. If they *believed* and were healed, then there was no reason why I could not accomplish the same outcome. I had to *believe*. I had to get hold of unwavering faith. It was the only way, if I wanted this to work for me, too.

Well, miraculously, after practicing everything I had learned, by September 2008, I had slowly weaned myself off most of my medications, leaving me with only one pill (an antidepressant). By January 2009, I had enrolled in an ultrasound college, and by February 2009, I finally became medication-*free*!

By December 2010, I graduated with honors (top four in my class) with an Associates of Science degree in Diagnostic Medical Sonography, and I had not gotten sick one day during my tenure in school. By the end of January 2011, I decided to specialize in the one organ that truly fascinated me, the heart. I took my National Boards and got registered as a diagnostic cardiac sonographer.

By May 2011, I began working in a cardiologist's office; however, my dream was to work in a hospital setting. By October

2012, my dream had come true: I obtained a position in a hospital. I still had not experienced any more bouts of depression, nor did any of the other personalities emerge again. Neither had any of the other medical ailments I had once suffered from interfere in my progress. However, the most miraculous gift of all was that I finally connected with God!

Finally, my confusing life began to change.

# Chapter 6:
# The Power of the Mind

*"That a man can change himself...*
*and master his own destiny*
*is the conclusion of every mind*
*who is wide-awake*
*to the power of right thought."*
*~ Christian D. Larson*

AFTER BETTER UNDERSTANDING ALL the turmoil in my life through this agonizing self-discovery process, and witnessing firsthand how I was able to break-free from such debilitating mental and medical conditions, I continued to put more pieces of the puzzle together. I became passionate in unraveling how influential the power of the mind really is. How it can work with you, as well as how it can work against you.

Through my journey of self-discovery, I learned how past patterns of behavior that were conditioned and created from my childhood poisoned my subconscious mind, reflecting in the detrimental stress and mental anguish I endured.

I began to learn that whatever our mind *believes*, it can achieve, whether it is through a negative or positive thought.

The most curious finding thus far, based on my own personal experience, leads me to consider that society has conditioned us to *believe* that certain diseases are normal and that without the intervention of medications, we cannot conquer our problem without it. However, doesn't medication just mask the problem and not actually correct the underlying cause that perhaps lies deep within our subconscious? Medication can help you stabilize, but, can it actually cure you?

If we can conquer how our minds think by enduring the self-discovery process, can we actually heal our diseases without medication? Maybe yes and maybe no, so I can only make claims on how it was "yes" for me.

So, as I educated myself through much more research after being introduced to *The Secret*, I learned that any disease basically derives from a mind that is not at ease. Can this basis alone originate from our past conditioning?

I assure you, that although I may not be the best person to conclude the answer to that question, I can admit to you that the power of the mind is much more complex than I can ever explain. I may not be a psychologist or have any professional schooling on the subject, nor am I here to proclaim that I truly understand how an individual's body chemistry works; however, my knowledge comes from my own experiences in the "school of life." I basically had no choice but to examine information that directly interrelated with what was happening to me personally in order to help me better understand how to control my mind versus it controlling me.

The most significant point in getting better, for me, was that I became aware that I was messed up. I accepted my past for what it was. I saw a destructive pattern of behavior—a pattern I wanted to liberate from, and I was finally able to see my future for what I wanted it to be and not for what I thought it was doomed to be based on my past conditioning.

Desiring a better life quickly propelled me to do something about it, but I still needed all the information I gathered to correlate with one another. It all needed to make sense to me before I could act on it. I really never had much schooling on the subject, and I never had anyone to really teach me anything except my forensic psychiatrist that helped me to understand behavioral psychology better. My persistence in looking things up and learning that way was what propelled me to figure things out in a way I never thought was possible.

My journey in the self-discovery process helped me to see where I was, how I got there, and it helped me learn where I wanted to go and how to get there. It was my road map to a complete recovery.

I first realized that something was seriously wrong after continuously experiencing moments when I would simply lose time. The best way I can attempt to help you better understand this feeling of losing time is similar to when you undergo surgery and receive general anesthesia that puts you out completely.

You know that feeling right before you go to sleep, when you remember everything? You remember the cold room with bright lights. You recall the nurses and doctors standing all around you, and then, all of a sudden, you wake up and it is all over. You feel as if time passed, something happened, but you remember nothing of the surgery itself, and you can feel the pain where you were cut open.

Well, that is just how I felt but without general anesthesia. So, whenever I woke up from this unexplainable state of mind, I experienced the worst headaches imaginable. I later found out they were called "switching headaches." For whatever reason, my subconscious mind did some funky stuff that caused me to momentarily forget that I was me, and I continued doing things that I was unaware of, claiming it was someone else. These so-called headaches were the result of intense switching between personalities. Pretty crazy stuff, right?

After several years of intense psychotherapy, I went on a journey to research the diagnoses I was plagued with to learn all about them. It was astonishing to read about characteristics I had displayed. Clearly, the doctors were correct with my diagnoses, but why was I like this? I struggled to figure out how I could change.

After I realized that something serious was happening in my mind, I was finally able to comprehend how powerful the mind was. My subconscious mind became so dominant that it did whatever the hell it wanted without my conscious consent.

I remember after my second suicide attempt, in my mid-twenties, I was asked why I was trying to hurt myself, and my spontaneous and automatic response was, "I am not trying to hurt myself, I am trying to keep myself from hurting!"

I even remember once telling my psychiatrist, "I am so afraid of myself. I feel as if I am living with my own killer, and I just don't know how to escape!"

Even though I was given a bunch of different medications, had undergone intensive psychotherapy and had consciously attempted to educate myself about these illnesses—and as much as I slowly improved throughout the years—I still experienced a lot of mental distress and anguish. I just didn't know how to liberate myself from all of it. This is when I told my doctor that I wanted to learn how to control my mind versus my mind controlling me.

I tried so hard to remain positive, to look for answers, yet I still couldn't control things that happened to me. Nobody was able to explain how I could control my mind. My doctors were there to help me cope and stabilize when in crisis, but not even they could tell me how to rid myself of this madness.

I just wanted it all to stop.

So, *The Secret* gave me a message that I was ready to hear. It just made so much sense after I'd been living a life that had never made sense before.

Basically, the message I got from *The Secret* was that everything works on conditioning: what you are conditioned to think on a daily basis is what your life becomes. This was when I first learned about the "Law of Attraction"; *what you think about, you bring about.*

Yet, I realized and acknowledged that *The Secret* was only a concept. You see, to actually learn to manifest what you want requires a lot more research, understanding, and determination. Although *The Secret* revealed a lot of things that made sense to me, how to apply them was a whole different ball game. My quest was to learn as much as I could and to habitually implement whatever teachings were necessary into my everyday life.

One of the first concepts in *The Secret* that made sense to me was how we live in a remnant of our thoughts. I understood this to mean that whatever thoughts we had in our past is what we live in now, in our current reality.

This was a powerful message for me. I began to put things into perspective and realized that every day in my past I had a lot of negative thoughts. Therefore, I was bringing all of that negativity into my current reality. Even though I struggled to do what others told me to do, "forget the past and just think positive," it just didn't work that easily for me. I'd make every attempt to think positively, but negativity seemed to lurk all around me. I just did not know how the whole "positive thinking" concept really worked. Sounded simple, but it was just not working for me at all.

I remember being infuriated when anyone even suggested that I wasn't thinking positively, because I tried so hard that it became strenuous to do. So telling me that I wasn't trying was like saying I was somehow weak, and that alone was insulting to me. I felt as if I was one of the strongest people on this earth, to exist with such insanity.

What I eventually understood from watching *The Secret* and doing more research was that it doesn't matter what you try to think with your conscious mind, it is the subconscious mind that makes things happen. However true this is, it was still a lot to absorb. These concepts pushed me to do further research and understand what the conscious and the subconscious mind really meant and how they relate to each other.

## The Conscious Mind

I found that being conscious is a state of being fully alert, aware, oriented, and responsive to the environment. I understood this to be the state when we are awake and are able to react to what occurs in our everyday lives. The conscious mind experiences all five senses: sight, sound, hearing, smell, and taste. We are aware of our surroundings and we know where we are. Once we are awakened from sleep, our conscious mind becomes alert again.

I also learned from Dr. Robert Anthony, a licensed psychotherapist and a hypnotherapist for more than thirty years as well as a best-selling author, that the conscious mind is the "thinker." With his analogy, I was able to correlate the "thinker" with who I am right now as I write—I am behaving as the "thinker."

I further understood from my research that the conscious mind's habitual thinking process creates memories that get stored up in the subconscious. I guess you could say that the conscious mind is like the programmer for the subconscious mind; at least, that is how I see it anyway.

## The Subconscious Mind

Now let's take a look at the subconscious mind. What is this, exactly? My general understanding is that it is a part of your mind that holds information. This is the place where we store memories of everything we see, hear, and experience during our lifetime whether it is negative or positive.

In my case, it is my *belief,* when my conscious mind (the thinker) experienced really bad and painful feelings; it locked them up in this subconscious storage area. It's as if I opened a drawer in my mind, shoved all of the painful stuff into it, and then closed the drawer.

Another way to look at the subconscious mind is as if it's a part of the brain that records information, similar to a tape recorder. These are recorded memories that originated from the "thinker" and/or the programmer, as I like to call it. These recorded messages can be recalled by the conscious mind at any given point, whether we are aware of the recordings or not. Apparently there are random circumstances that may occur in our lives that can force these recordings to surface, something I learned are called "triggers".

I was grateful to learn that these painful recorded messages stored in our subconscious "mind drawers" can be deleted and replaced with new, more pleasant recordings. The trick was learning how to find the "delete" and "re-record" buttons. Yet if you don't admit these negative recorded messages exist, regardless of what they may be, you will never have the ability to change them—that I was convinced of. I learned that denial is a culprit from acquiring success with this reprogramming and/or reconditioning process.

## How Did This Relate to My Personal Life?

I associated this to my multiple personality disorder. I knew that I had a lot of traumatic and painful recorded memories locked up in my subconscious "mind drawers" that my conscious mind didn't want to think about. It was like some sort of internal self-help mechanism that I'd developed over time. I obviously became aware of this fact during my psychotherapy sessions. My forensic psychiatrist was an excellent teacher in helping me make sense of this reality.

I came to the understanding that after so many years of harboring painful memories, my subconscious mind apparently became overloaded and had no room to store any more recordings. It's similar to a computer when it runs out of memory; you just cannot save anything else to it.

This prevented the conscious mind from storing any more new pain; now it had to keep the pain all for itself. Unfortunately, the conscious mind didn't know how to deal with this pain, and the moment it felt any new pain coming on, it just shut down. This allowed the subconscious recordings to surface and play for all to hear.

Over a period of fourteen years, this became a big problem. No matter how much I may have improved with medication and psychotherapy, I had so much deep-rooted pain that it just kept chasing itself around, like a dog chasing after its own tail.

I was able to reason that my ability to function fairly well for many years was because as long as I had these "mind drawers" to put painful memories in, my conscious mind was okay. Although I would freak out a bit whenever I felt emotional pain, I would immediately shove the pain into these "mind drawers," and then everything would be just fine again. Once there was no place to put the new pain, though, my entire internal system began to malfunction. Then, shutting down was the only way that my conscious mind knew how to escape the pain.

It became apparent, throughout the years, that after experiencing some type of severe emotional anxiety, stress, or abuse, I would just drop like a ton of bricks—just like when I was found slumped over the steering wheel of my car.

As another example, an incident occurred after a very stressful argument I had with my second husband over the phone. Consequently, after this phone conversation, my son found me unconscious not knowing what had happened, so he immediately called 911. He was terrified. He later admitted to me that he thought I was dying, because he could not wake me up.

When the paramedics arrived, they made every attempt to wake me. They called out my name and vigorously shook my shoulders. They put ammonia under my nose, and they dug their knuckles hard into the center of my chest (my sternum), none of which roused me.

The irony was that I could feel and hear everything. It was as if I was locked-up in my mind someplace, and I couldn't get out. My mind kept saying, "Stop hurting me; stop hurting me. Please stop hurting me, please," because the intense digging of their knuckles on my sternum was so excruciatingly painful. Nonetheless, I couldn't seem to move; I couldn't speak; I couldn't tell them how much they were hurting me.

"I am trapped in here. Please help me get out, please let me OUT!" I continued to cry in my mind.

It was as if I were paralyzed. I couldn't tell them to stop putting that awful smell under my nose either. Yet I was able to hold my breath for moments at a time, to keep out that suffocating odor. How weird was that? The only indications to the paramedics that I could hear and feel were the tears streaming down my face.

Another time, I remember slowly coming back to consciousness and I could hear people speaking. I then felt an awful stinging pain in my wrists, but although I could feel this pain and I could hear people's voices, I again could not move. I could not yell-out how painful it was. Yet, again, I felt trapped within my own mind.

I then remember a voice say, "She must really be out, because this numbing medicine is very painful and she hasn't even flinched." It was an Emergency room physician that was getting ready to stitch up wounds on my wrists that were self-inflicted.

Those were moments where I suspect Jenny O had tried to kill me, and then Katherine would just come-out, shut-down and take over, paralyzing me.

These things that happened were so troubling for me and difficult for anyone else to comprehend. There are many more stories that I can tell, but that would probably take-up an entire book in itself, so I will stick to just these examples for now.

Intense psychotherapy helped reveal the how, what, and why all the personalities were created. This is what I mean when I say that I would just shut down. It is still very hard to speak about these personalities, because the truth is, they were really all me.

I still wonder why my mind decided to split and create these personalities. I have heard many stories of people who endured much more troubling and horrific abuse in their lives than I did, yet they didn't suffer from multiple personality disorder. Why this became my method of coping will always be a mystery to me. I guess the important thing is simply to accept it for what it is and continue with my healing process.

After learning more about the conscious and subconscious mind, I realized that these so-called personalities were actually the painful recorded memories that were shoved away in those "mind drawers." When my conscious mind became overloaded, these subconscious "mind drawers" opened up, and the painful recordings just poured-out. This is why I reasoned that my conscious mind simply went away, and my subconscious came out to play for all to hear.

I understand this must be difficult for you to fully comprehend, so imagine how I felt living this kind of life. At that point, my mind was only doing whatever it needed to do to survive. I just didn't know how to control it. My life was at the mercy of my mind.

It is still hard for me to truly understand how the entire MPD/DID condition works, because many psychiatrists also have difficulty understanding my disorder. Some of them have never even met a person with MPD/DID; therefore, it is very difficult for many to even acknowledge that such a condition even exists.

Because I lived this kind of life, I eventually realized that I needed to erase those ugly recordings from my head. I needed to empty out those "mind drawers" and start putting pleasant recordings in place of the negativity, because if I didn't find a way, I was going to die, without a doubt.

I felt as if a cancer was slowly eating away at my brain, and I needed to find the cure. This alone was a journey for me. I needed to educate myself, because it was obvious how corrupt and powerful my mind had become, so I continued my learning expedition and discovered information about brain-wave frequencies.

## Brain-Wave Frequencies

During further research, I learned that our conscious and subconscious minds work on different brain-wave frequencies. These frequencies are called alpha, beta, delta, and theta. I will briefly review these as I learned to understand them. I guess it doesn't matter whether I perfectly grasped the logistics of everything; what matters is that my reasoning and "*belief*" in it was enough to propel me into getting better.

This is the first time I ever discussed this with anyone, so most of my interpretation came from reading and simply figuring it out on my own. I looked at several Internet websites before I could get in touch with my own perceptions. These websites all contain slightly different information, but I will do my best to relay the information in the way that I understand it. I urge you to do your homework, too, should you still have any questions after my explanations.

## Beta Frequency

The beta frequency occurs when we are wide awake. The frequency generated during this time can range from 13 to 30HZ. If you are operating within this range of frequency, it is said to be associated with peak *concentration, heightened alertness, good hand-eye coordination, and visual activity*. This has something to do with neurons in our brains that are able to fire rapidly in succession, which supposedly helps us to achieve peak performance when we are awake. In this state of mind, we are able to absorb new ideas and solve problems. Therefore, this frequency occurs during our conscious state of mind.

## Alpha Frequency

The alpha frequency is the brain wave that allows wakeful relaxation, visualization, and creativity to occur. This brain activity is much slower than the rapid beta (conscious) state of mind. Alpha generates a frequency between 7 and 13 HZ.

When you are truly relaxed, the alpha state subsequently slows you down, and your awareness expands. This is when your visualized creativity begins to flow and your fears can be eliminated.

A type of alpha training called biofeedback is the most commonly recommended treatment to reduce stress. Alpha brain waves are a much deeper state of consciousness. My hope was that perhaps I could experience a sense of peace and well-being in this brain-wave frequency. If only I could reduce my anxiety level, then this would be a big accomplishment.

I was fascinated to learn that the alpha frequency was also known as a resonant (vibrating) frequency, which is the same frequency as the earth's electromagnetic field. It might be cool if I could attune myself to the earth's electromagnetic field, and the Universe's as well.

## Theta Frequency

The theta brain-wave frequency occurs during deep relaxation and meditation; in this mental state, you have access to stored, long-forgotten memories. This state of mind has brain waves of a much slower frequency, between 3 and 7HZ. Your brain activity slows down almost to a sleep state, but not quite fully into sleep.

The theta state of mind is where the magic happens. This is the place where behavior modification can occur. In the theta level, we have heightened receptivity and inspiration, and flashes of dreamlike images occur. By experiencing this low brain wave frequency, you can reach the deep state of meditation that I kept learning was so powerful. This is a state in which you almost feel as if you are floating freely, as your mind *expands beyond the boundaries of your body.*

I realized that if I could meditate in this brain-wave frequency and reach this gateway to learning and memory, it might just be the place where I could access and delete old memories and teach my brain new ones. It really made a lot of sense to me. Clearly, I needed to learn to enter this level of meditation with a controlled state of mind.

## Delta Frequency

The delta frequency is the slowest of all of the brain waves. The range of frequency generated during this state of mind is 0 to 3HZ. Delta is the brain-wave frequency that is called the subconscious. We enter this state of mind during deep sleep. It is also a beneficial place for the body to heal. It is where intuition arises. When you access your subconscious, you can clear away what your conscious mind put in there, because it is a place of pure empowerment.

This is only a brief summary of what I learned. Yet I came to realize that if I could relax enough, while controlling my thoughts as I slowed down my brain-wave frequency, perhaps I could actually begin the healing process. If I could reach these alpha and theta levels and access my imagination and creative abilities before I entered the delta level (the place of healing), perhaps I could finally accomplish my goal of eliminating all of those painful memories that had been locked inside for so many years. This was my *belief*.

After learning all of this, I specifically remember watching a part of the movie *The Secret* where a man gets a tape recorder with earphones, lies under a tree, closes his eyes, and just listens. I don't know what he was listening to, but I began to realize that I had to listen to something too. I needed help in shifting the negative thoughts in my alpha and theta levels to positive ones, so that I could change and heal my subconscious (delta level) programming.

I was open to these new ideas and was relentless in my search for the right message that would allow this shift to take place in my mind.

That is when I found the amazing meditation/manifestation audio online that helped me to learn to relax with breathing exercises. I had tried numerous other meditation audios, but this particular audio really helped me. After I listened to it for a few days, my mind was able to stop focusing on day-to-day frustrations or thinking about things from my past. I was finally able to quieten my mind and project how I wanted to feel in the present moment.

As I lay there every night, I entered a state of pure serenity. I envisioned myself leading a healthy life. My sense of imagination became vivid and alive. I could feel the sensation of being healed, an exuberant feeling that made me tingle all over, because now my creativity was blossoming. It was as if I were still awake but no longer in this same world. It was like entering a whole different dimension. I literally felt as if I was floating someplace outside of my body. I felt the happiness of being in that magical place, even if in reality, it was only in my mind. I even remember imagining my loved ones standing around me, congratulating me for reaching such a healthy state in my life.

Every time I reached the end of the audiotape, it helped me be grateful for receiving such an amazing healing. This audiotape also guided me to give all of my gratitude to God for receiving this wonderful healing. I remember that when I got that tingling feeling all over my body, I *believed* I was somehow connecting with that higher Divine spiritual entity everyone proclaims to exist in the Universe. This was all still so new to me, but it surely felt good *believing* it was all true.

I don't think there are enough words to describe what an amazing place that was. When the twenty-minute audio was nearing the end, I simply didn't want to let it go. I didn't want to leave this magical place. It was such an amazing experience that tears of joy rolled down my face, and my smile reached ear to ear as I meditated. It didn't feel as though my entire journey lasted only twenty minutes, because time seemed to be irrelevant during this incredible adventure. Of course, the audio teaches you to eventually let go and know that what you have asked for has been given.

After thanking God for letting me experience such a beautiful moment, I always felt a sense of peace in my heart and was able to fall asleep easily. One thing is for sure: when morning came, I couldn't wait until the next evening when I could watch *The Secret* movie again and listen to my favorite audio. This allowed me to go back to my happy place, where I *believed* the Spirit of God was ever-present, reminding me that everything I had researched and learned was real. My sense of hope and faith just seemed to grow stronger and stronger.

I may not be 100 percent correct with my theory, but all I can do is try to make sense of what happened to me, basing it on all of the research I did and by putting the pieces together from the memories that surfaced during my extensive therapy sessions.

Regardless of whether others accept my theory to be true or not, I *believed* that my theory was correct, so even if just my *belief* in this theory was enough to propel me to wellness, then the philosophy I've read about the "Law of Belief" is 100 percent correct: *that whatever is in your **belief** system whether with feeling and conviction or not becomes your reality*, hence the correlation with "The Law of Attraction".

I also learned that the Bible reveals in Mark 11:24 (AKJV):

> *"Therefore I say unto you, What things soever ye desire, when ye pray, **believe** that ye receive them, and ye shall have them."*

With this reasoning and *belief*, I began reconditioning how my subconscious mind thought and felt. It seemed that I was slowly deleting those negative recordings and replacing them with positive ones. Although the feelings I had experienced during meditation led me to *believe* that I was making a definite connection with God, I still needed to learn more about Him. So, during this time, I also found myself studying about God and His energy. I will later elaborate more about my findings in reference.

I can honestly say that this was truly the beginning of my awakening and without a doubt the beginning of my entire medical healing process.

I finally saw a glimpse of light emerge from a crack in my dark world. I slowly began to squeeze through this ever so slightly slither of light eagerly fighting to escape. I was gradually learning how to break-free from the confinement of my depressing and twisted mind: a place that held me captive for most of my life. I felt like a butterfly breaking out from its cocoon with the most beautiful, radiant and vibrant colors, ready to spread my wings and fly in a world I'd always dreamed of exploring.

I found that the power of the subconscious mind is beyond incredible. It is only through awareness, education, understanding and acceptance that anyone can overcome destructive mental conditioning. You don't have to suffer from a mental illness to experience detrimental effects from past conditioning. I just want to show you through my own personal experience that it is possible to overcome these remnants from the past.

You too can experience change in your life. So at this point I want to ask you, "Is there something you want to change in your life? If so, how bad is your desire to change?"

# Chapter 7:
# Change Doesn't Happen Overnight

*"We are what we repeatedly do.*
*Excellence, then, is not an act, but a habit."*
*~ Aristotle*

MY MIRACLE MEDICAL HEALING did not happen overnight. It just doesn't work that way. I was surely grateful for this new audio I was listening to. I *believed* it was my last hope. I enjoyed how it made me feel, so I planned to stick with it. I needed a change in my life that bad, so I continued on this new mission.

I began practicing all I had learned every day beginning in April 2008. I also decided to stop seeing my psychiatrist during this time. I wanted to do this all alone; I didn't even tell my family and friends what I did every night. I just didn't want any outside influence. I didn't want anyone telling me I could not do this. I didn't want any negative feedback from anyone. I didn't want to hear constructive criticism, either. I just needed to be left alone to allow myself to consciously reach these brain-wave frequencies without any outside interference whatsoever. I needed to continue looking inward versus looking for exterior relief that never brought about permanent results. I also needed to *believe* that the amazing tingling feeling I experienced during meditation was some sort of connection I was making with God's amazing spiritual energy. So this journey became solely one between God and me.

After a few weeks of doing this, when it was time to take my meds, for the first time, I just didn't want to take them anymore.

Now, these were meds that I hadn't been able to sleep without, let alone live without. I was also aware that because my body was dependent on those pills, stopping them abruptly would probably force my body into withdrawal. I even remember my forensic psychiatrist warning me not to stop my medication suddenly, because it could propel me into a huge setback. So, after I had been meditating for a few weeks, I decided to wean myself off these pills slowly by taking six pills a day, instead of seven. I seemed to do just fine that first night and for the following week as well.

I must stress that I do not recommend that anyone simply stop taking his or her medication. It is important for you to understand that I was only doing what came naturally for me. I didn't stop taking my medication because of a rebellious state of mind, as I had when I was younger. I was fully aware of my feelings and had become extremely vigilant and able to detect what made me feel good versus what made me feel bad. I had been very dedicated and careful during this long journey.

With that said, I continued watching the movie and listening to the audio and thanking God each time for my healing. About a week later, I removed another pill from my daily dose and did very well with that. I continued this process every few weeks. I removed another pill only when I was 100 percent sure that I was stable with the newly lowered dose.

By September 2008, I was down to just one antidepressant and was sleeping like a baby. I had not experienced any highs or lows and had not felt depressed nor did any personalities emerge. All I knew was that every night I was going to my happy place before I went to sleep. I had dreamless nights or, at least, no dreams that I could remember. The following morning I would wake up happy, and I tried to do productive things throughout the day. This gave me hope and even more motivation to continue on this new path of healing.

For whatever reason, though, my mind was afraid to stop taking this one last antidepressant. The only way I can describe it

is that this antidepressant was like my thin security b]
this was just the beginning, and I wasn't going to allow fear to get
in the way of a full recovery, so I continued my daily practices.

By the following January 2009, I came across a book called
*Zero Limits* written by Joel Vital, one of *The Secret* participants.
This book was about Joe's journey in meeting a psychiatrist in
Hawaii by the name of Ihaleakala Hew Len, Ph.D., who helped heal
an entire ward full of mentally ill criminals without ever
consulting with them. I thought this story was beyond incredible. I
became intrigued with this book and wanted to know more,
especially since it had to do with the mental health topic. So, I
planned to purchase the book.

During this time, I remember that whenever I spoke to my
son, he was the one who always made negative comments, and I
was the one making positive comments. Right before his twenty-
seventh birthday, he said to me, "Damn, Mom, I am the one who
introduced you to *The Secret*, and here you are the positive one
and me the negative one."

I still wasn't into reading books, per se, because all of the
research I had done was online, so I decided to purchase the book
*Zero Limits*, and have it mailed to my son. I told him that I wanted
him to read it, and if he felt it was worthy of reading, then he could
give it to me, and I'd agree to read it too. I trusted his judgment
because he'd made an excellent choice in giving *The Secret* to me.
Since my son had gone through so much with me and my mental
distress, and he, too, had experienced depression in his life, I
hoped that it would be a positive experience for him.

Well, lo and behold, he read the book and called me up to
say, "Mom, this book is amazing, and I am not giving you my copy. I
have purchased another one and I am having it mailed to you."

So I read the book and learned something very interesting
that correlated with the subconscious mind reprogramming

journey I had ventured on. It is my understanding that after you enter the subconscious mind, it takes the information you programmed there and sends it to a much higher level of consciousness called the "superconscious," which apparently has a direct correlation with Divine energy.

In summation, I understood the following as a result of my intense research: The thoughts implanted during the alpha and theta frequency levels, which ultimately resonate in the delta level, not only reprogram the subconscious mind, but these thoughts then travel to the "superconscious," which has a direct link to that amazing supernatural Divine energy that I longed to find. I understood that this is how "what you really want" is relayed to the Universe—to my God, whom I *believe* is the creator of the Universe, the ultimate source of answers to our prayers. Once again, helping me associate it with the "Law of Attraction"; *what you think about, you bring about.*

It was an incredible revelation for me. You see, all this time I had been doing everything I needed to do with the audio to reprogram my subconscious, I always felt I was connecting with God somehow, yet I wasn't sure that this was really happening. I just blindly went by *belief*, faith and feeling. So, the information I got from *Zero Limits* gave me that last piece of the puzzle to help me realize my suspicion was correct: I was actually connecting with God. That is why my prayers were finally being answered like never before. I was so happy to learn this sequence of events! It was the breakthrough I had been longing to find. It all made perfect sense to me now.

I also began a very interesting practice that was mentioned in *Zero Limits*. The practice consisted of repeating the following words: "I'm sorry, please forgive me, thank You, I love You." I won't go into detail about what it means, but it is basically a phrase I learned to express to my Divine or Higher Self or God.

Up until that point, the meditation seemed to be working, and if it is true that our subconscious mind has a direct energized link to God through our superconscious; and if it is true that we attract everything in our lives, as *The Secret* claims, and that God forgives, as people proclaim, then this saying might just work in conjunction with what I was already doing. I needed to *believe* that God would forgive all of the bad that had happened to me, all of the bad things I had allowed to happen to me in my past. I needed to *believe* that God could feel all of the love and gratitude that resonated within my soul and how genuinely my faith in Him had grown.

I also reasoned that perhaps whenever there was something negative in my life that I didn't mean to attract, I could close my eyes and say these powerful words to flush all of the negativity away. This seemed to be more of a faith-based healing technique, so I *believed* in its power and decided to implement it in my everyday life.

Basically, I did not "hope" it would work, but I *"believed"* it would. Most people "hope" something will work, but aren't quite sure it will; therefore, deep down their skeptic mind doesn't really *"believe"* that it will work. Then when something doesn't work, they can prove their skepticism was correct all along.

Anyhow, I found myself *"believing"* that these delightful words would work and began saying them over and over again, day in and day out, numerous times a day. I would just close my eyes and allow myself to drift into that magical spiritual dimension. I uttered those words with all of the faith that vibrated inside every cell of my being. I even remember getting a tingling feeling after saying it, *believing* that this was God's spiritual energy resonating within me and responding that He heard me. I *believed* it was His way of letting me know everything was going to be okay. So I embraced the tingling as if it was a comforting hug from God.

As a result, every night before I was ready to take that last antidepressant pill, I would say, "I'm sorry, please forgive me, thank You, and I love You." Then, for whatever reason, one night I looked at that pill and just did not want to take it anymore, and so I stopped. I am proud to say that I have been completely medication-free since February 2009.

Now, as I go back and relive all of this, it gives me proof of how much power the mind has. How powerful it is to reprogram your subconscious by quieting the mind through meditation, erasing the old recorded messages that were implanted years ago, and replacing them with new recordings through the brain-wave frequency theory. Finally, I found the "delete" and "re-record buttons."

I began to realize why the point made in *The Secret* is so true: how we live in the remnants of our thoughts. I habitually did all of these new practices every single day, day in and day out, month in and month out. Eventually, I began to live in the remnants of my new positive thoughts. Ultimately, both my conscious and my subconscious mind were working together in unison, and I was finally able to communicate the right message to God. No more pain, no more depression, no more highs and lows, and most importantly, no more personality switching. I was finally whole, I was finally healed, and I had finally awakened to the miraculous powers of the Universe, as *The Secret* suggests is possible!

I went from being a crazy bat out of hell, taking endless amounts of medication, attempting suicide countless times and being hospitalized over and over, to being a happy, mentally healthy, medication-free, productive member of society who was enrolled in college. And this was just in the first ten months of putting into action the tools I'd acquired from my research after I learned the concepts in *The Secret*.

I remember that in January 2009, I decided to go see my forensic psychiatrist again. I finally made an appointment to go and tell him everything that I had done, along with describing the results in detail. This was right before I weaned myself off that last antidepressant.

When he walked into the office, I said, "I am so happy and want to share my happiness with you."

"Wow, it's great to see you again!" he replied. "What is making you so happy?"

With a big smile on my face, I eagerly told him, "It's *The Secret*. You know about *The Secret*?"

With a puzzled look, he said, "No, I don't know about *The Secret*."

So, I explained everything to him, and he became rather curious. He went online and looked it up, and there was a website where you could watch the first twenty minutes of the movie for free. We just sat there together as he quietly watched.

When it was over, he had a great big smile on his face and said, "Wow . . . that is some very interesting stuff."

By the end of the session, when he was ready to write me the prescription, I said, "No, I don't need medication anymore. I am down to one antidepressant and I have a lot left over, plus I still have some refills left. I hope to wean myself off that one soon."

He was shocked, but pleasantly surprised. He was also thrilled to hear I had enrolled in college.

Then, after I graduated college, got a job in my new career and moved into my new apartment, on December 9, 2011, I went to pay my forensic psychiatrist another visit. This time when he walked in, I said in a cheerful tone of voice, "I didn't come to see you because I need you. I'm here because I missed you. I am completely healed!"

He was so happy for me. We spoke at great length about my healing journey, and he was beyond mesmerized with the results.

At the end of the session, he walked me out of the office, because I was his last patient of the day. I told him I probably wouldn't see him again. I knew his time was very valuable, and I had to stop interfering with his journey of helping people who really needed it most.

He hugged me tight and said, "Jenny, you can come back and visit me any time. I'm very proud of you."

We then parted ways.

My psychiatrist was not only my doctor, but he also became my mentor and my best friend. He is the only human being who has ever understood me and never abandoned me. There aren't enough words to describe the knowledge he gave me in fourteen years of consistent psychotherapy. I will be eternally grateful to him for helping me to stay alive long enough to figure it all out.

I was so happy with the new recordings in my head that repeated, "I am healed. I am healthy. I am successful. I am worthy. I am happy. I am love." I finally found myself smiling all the time . . . and not only during my meditations.

Here is very powerful quote that I want to share with you:

> *"Choice is a Limitation. . . . We can appeal to Divinity who knows our personal blueprint, for healing of all thoughts and memories that are holding us back at this time."*
> —*Morrnah Simeona*

I reasoned that Divinity is God, the creator of the Universe. He is the only one who knows our blueprint and the only one who can truly heal us. As the saying goes,

> *"If you can **believe** it, you can achieve it"*
> —*Napoleon Hill*

Another famous quote by Albert Einstein that I find fascinating states:

> *"Imagination is more important than knowledge. Knowledge is limited, imagination encircles the world."*

I came to the understanding that you can gain knowledge from all of the things I have spoken about thus far, but only by implementing this knowledge in your everyday life and engaging in creative imagination can you change your own personal world.

I have confidence that if more people can understand the concept regarding the power of imagination, the powers of the subconscious, the powers of the Universe that all derive from the Power of God, regardless from what walk of life they come from and regardless of what their core *belief* system may be, they will be one step ahead of the game.

I even found where the bible declares:

> *"And the* LORD *said, Behold, the people is one, and they have all one language; and this they begin to do: and now nothing will be restrained from them, which they have **imagined** to do." (Genesis 11:6 (AKJV)*

You see, it is my *belief* that we all have the capability to speak the same language without originating from the same culture, because we all have the same thing in common: we all have the same creative power that originates from God. We all have a subconscious and superconscious. The question is, do we actually know how to tap into this higher than life entity effectively through the power of our own imagination? Do we know how to quiet our minds for long enough to not only pray, imagine and ask, but can we patiently wait for the answer that will ultimately arise from within? As spoken in Psalm 46:10(AKJV):

> *"Be still, and know that I am God: I will be exalted among the heathen, I will be exalted in the earth."*

I learned through internet research that exalted means *raised or elevated* and heathen means *an unconverted member of a people or nation that does not acknowledge the God of the Bible.* So my interpretation and perception of this scripture is that God will reveal Himself to the non-believers and will be raised and/or elevated by them on earth, once they learn how to quiet their minds and know that He is God.

Why don't people quiet their minds more often? It is my opinion that most people just have trouble practicing this because they find it difficult to let go of their personal thoughts; thus, not allowing God to bring upon the answer by way of supernatural thought that filters through their superconscious.

My conclusion comes from my own past experience. Not only did I not know how to quiet my mind, nobody really ever taught me how, despite my psychiatrist's willingness to teach me. Most of the time I idly *believed* it was impossible to quiet my racing thoughts; therefore, my *belief* came true. It wasn't until I began to *"believe"* that it "was" possible that it "became" possible. If you *believe* you can, then you will, and if you *believe* you can't, then you won't.

I encourage everyone to read the books I have thus far mentioned and learn from the wisdom in them. I only wish I had read them earlier, but it worked out well anyway. For me, *The Secret* was the true life changer, because it propelled me to do a lot of research online that I'd never thought to attempt before. As a result, an amazing spiritual shift occurred within me. Afterwards,

*Zero Limits* helped to finalize my healing by helping me understand how we connect with Divine energy, and scriptures from the bible helped me confirm my new spiritual walk with God was right on track.

Despite all I have learned thus far, I still consider myself a newborn in this incredible supernatural world, where the powers of God Whom created the Universe reside.

All I can say for certain is that it works. It really and truly works. I can honestly attest that there were times when—I won't lie—I fell short of doing these practices, and sometimes still do. And you know what? Suddenly, things don't pan-out as I want them to. Then I'll catch myself and begin again, and then everything begins to flow; just as it had before.

Although sometimes I still fall off the wagon and fail to remember how powerful our imagination is, I guess it's all becoming more natural for me now. Apparently, because I have been practicing for so long, there are more positive thoughts than negative ones implanted in my subconscious mind. For this reason, it is my *belief* that no matter how many times I may falter, it is easy to pick myself up and simply start right where I left off. Nobody is perfect, and I don't profess to be. After all, I am still a work in progress!

I just wanted to stress how change doesn't happen overnight. If you can imagine yourself the way you want to be and the way God sees you, change will happen, without a shadow of a doubt. You just need to *believe*. So if you have found yourself in a dark place in life, I can corroborate that this is definitely one way to the light.

So, now I would like to ask you to take a good look at your life. Have you figured out yet what it is that you want to change? If so, what is it, and how bad do you desire to change?

# Chapter 8:
# Where is He?

*"...the Spirit of God lives in you..."*
*Romans 8:9(AKJV)*

AS I WENT ALONG ON my journey—learning about the conscious, the subconscious, all of the different brain-wave frequencies and the superconscious—at the same time I was asking questions about God. It just happened that all of the information I gathered seemed to fit together like pieces of a puzzle.

I realize that the subject of God, the Universe, spirituality and/or religion is very controversial for many people. It was for me, too, for the first forty-six years of my life, especially when I was so sick. I just could not understand where this miraculous God was, and why He was leaving me alone to suffer so much. Why, when I called out for His help, didn't I feel help arriving? "Where is He," I asked with disbelief?

As a result, I was a big skeptic about the existence of God. So, although I have elaborated a great deal about my newly found connection with God, I want to further explain my true journey in knowing Him better. It was quite difficult at first to make that connection I have, thus far, spoken about; however, I am grateful for allowing myself to reason, let go and accept this newly found journey of mine.

To go back to my upbringing for a moment, I can honestly say that I was raised by non-believers or, at least, what I perceive to be non-believers. So learning about God and His existence was quite a journey for me—let alone being able to make sense of it as an adult.

Although I was baptized as a baby in the Catholic Church, I don't recall ever being educated about God, Christ, or the church. I do remember that as a young girl, perhaps at the ages of six, seven, or eight, I had friends in school who went to church. Some of my friends got to do what was called their "Communion," where they wore pretty white dresses and looked like angels and princesses. When I saw the pictures they brought to school, I knew that I wanted to look like an angel and feel like a princess too.

I even remember asking my parents, "When are we going to church?" I don't remember getting a positive response.

Throughout my life, I remember that I wanted to know more about God and I wanted to go to church, but I never had the opportunity during my earlier years. I felt fortunate when I was married the first time, because I was able to get married in a church.

Although the Catholic Church would not marry us, because I was too young and had not received my sacraments, I was able to get married in a Methodist church. I really didn't know the difference between one church and the other, nor of their personal rituals. I simply wanted to get married in a church and wear a white dress. I still wanted to look like an angel and feel like a princess.

I remember the first time I entered the living room of my in-laws' house. They had a picture hanging on the wall of my sister-in-law dressed in her white clothes at her Communion. I remember thinking, "Wow, she got to do that! I always wanted to do that too!"

I also remember how my husband, at the time, helped me learn to pray "The Our Father." Now I know that it is actually called "The Lord's Prayer," and he also taught me to pray the "Hail Mary." I remember going to bed every night and saying those two prayers with my husband until I eventually memorized them. I really didn't know much about what it all meant, I just needed to learn how to pray. It made me feel good.

Years passed, and once in a while we went to a local Catholic church, like maybe for Easter. Then my sister-in-law got married in a Catholic Church, and that was very cool. I learned that God was our spiritual Father in Heaven and that this higher-than-life, powerful being had brought us His Son Jesus, to wash away and rectify our sins. I was told that God, Jesus, and the Holy Spirit were all one. Other than that, I didn't know much. Then, at the age of twenty-three, unfortunately, I got divorced and was left to raise my three-year-old son alone.

Nonetheless, around the time I was initially diagnosed with clinical depression, in my mid-twenties, I knew that I still needed to learn more about God. I hoped to find peace with Him, versus taking medication, which I had refused to do. Yet some things puzzled me about the whole religion thing. There was supposedly one God and one Jesus, but there were countless different denominational churches. All of these churches evidently read the same Bible, yet they all followed God so differently. That didn't make sense to me.

I remember trying to read the Bible to better understand everything, but it was written in what I perceived to be a foreign language. Not having good concentration or comprehension skills, I just put the Bible down and gave up on reading it. So I remained confused about this subject.

I even remember going with my young son to all kinds of churches, looking for answers to my questions. I went to Catholic churches, Baptist churches, Methodist churches, and so on. Yet, I was still lost when I tried to understand how they all operated so differently—not to mention learning that people of the Jewish faith didn't even *believe* that Jesus was the Messiah. So, who was right?

I just never really felt as if I fit in anywhere. The whole religion thing never made any sense to me. Everyone had their own rituals and their own *belief* systems, and if you didn't do it their way, then you were going to Hell. This alone scared the daylights out of me.

I mean, who was I to *believe*? I thought church would be a place full of love and hope, not a place of fear. I just became more confused, because none of these churches ever fulfilled me. I didn't know which group to follow, because all I wanted to learn was how to follow God. So, since none of these churches gave me any satisfaction, I decided that I wasn't going to church anymore. I even wondered whether this was why my parents never wanted to go to church either.

I remember telling a friend, "I don't understand any of this. I *believe* that God speaks to us through our hearts, so why should I have to go to church?"

Why I felt this way, I don't know.

Yet I still *believed* that some kind of higher power existed, and deep down I *believed* in Jesus too, because I considered myself a Christian. I finally decided, however, that church just wasn't for me.

Now we come to my epiphany, how I began to understand the whole God subject better. Needless to say, the book *The Secret* refers only to the Universe, because it rarely uses the term God in any context. The author does speak a lot about how the Universe is energy and the Universe gives you everything you want. All you have to do is ask, and the Universe will give it to you. People at church would also say that all you have to do is ask God, and He will answer your prayers. So the only way I could rationalize it in the beginning was that God and the Universe must be the same entity. The more I watched this movie, the more I gradually made sense of this confusing concept.

As I listened to the ideas expressed in *The Secret*, I picked up on other interesting things too. For example, the author kept talking about how "we" are "all" made up of energy.

"So what exactly is energy?" I wondered. From the movie and book, I came to understand how energy is something you can never create or destroy. So if there is no explanation on the creation of God, nor how anyone can destroy Him, then God must be made up of energy. I then concluded that this energy is what is referred to as the Spirit of God, a large energy field that resides in the Universe.

I then remembered how people say that you can have ever-lasting life after death. So what exactly is it about us that lives on after death? There must be something about us that also cannot be destroyed. Hence, I came to the realization that we too must be made-up of energy, like God. So putting two and two together, I began to reason that if we are made-up of energy just like God, Who cannot be destroyed, then perhaps our energy is also a Spirit like God. So I determined that we are both an energy field that exists in the Universe. I finally began to see God as a large energy field and us as a smaller energy field.

I finally began to realize that perhaps I had been wrong this entire time in looking for God in the outside world by attempting to follow people that I thought knew more than me. Perhaps God was living in this amazing energized spiritual world that in actuality existed within me, in a place I had access to, and all because I, too, was an energized spirit.

During this time, I was still researching the conscious mind, the subconscious, the superconscious and brain-wave frequencies, so I had a great deal of information to process at once. It was like a jigsaw puzzle, I had a lot of pieces and all I needed was to fit the pieces together to understand the full picture.

I was truly convinced that we all have the ability to connect with this larger energy field—but exactly "how" was still my passionate inquiry.

My reasoning first began with the fascinating way we can connect with other human beings by using a telephone line. For example, if you want to talk to your parents and ask them for something—like a weed-whacker, for example—you can sit in your living room all day long and ask for it. They surely can't hear you, though, unless you pick up the telephone and actually call them to ask for it. Through this type of communication line, you can actually speak to your earthly parents. Isn't this the only way they can hear what you want and agree to give it to you?

So, the possibility that there was a better method to communicate with our spiritual Heavenly Father became very real for me. My mind was certainly full of weeds that I needed to remove, so I had to learn how to communicate with God to ask Him for a weed-whacker. This is when the alpha, theta, delta frequency levels, the subconscious and superconscious theory, made even more sense to me. Surely, this was the spiritual communication line I needed to learn to use.

Once I began to grasp these concepts a little better, I reverted back to *The Secret*. I remember James Ray having an interesting analogy about Aladdin and his lamp. This story is about how Aladdin rubs a lamp and out pops a Genie that grants him 3 wishes. So, the basic point on how Aladdin asks the Genie and is granted his wishes, apparently the same holds true between us and God. However, God obviously isn't a Genie, so the three wish limit doesn't apply, as scripture even says that all you have to do is ask and it will be given, right? There is no mention that you can only ask God three times. Anyhow, this Genie analogy alone helped me better understand that regardless how you put it, the concept regarding asking is the same.

You see, in the same way that Aladdin happened to communicate with the Genie by rubbing the lamp, I was gradually learning how to communicate with God through my subconscious. Once I rubbed my superconscious with unwavering faith and *belief*, my healing process became possible. I was finally able to clearly relay the desires of my heart that in turn allowed the Lord to see my pure and humbled soul. My wish of being healed was granted. My faith and *belief* was as strong as is stated in the faith expressed in Jeremiah 17:14 (AKJV):

> *"Heal me, O Lord, and I shall be healed; save me, and I shall be saved."*

As a result, our Heavenly Father granted my wish, and He healed me.

It became my *belief* that the important thing isn't "what" you ask for, but "how" you ask for it. I realized that with the proven scientific explanations I had learned in conjunction with faith-based *belief* revealed a remarkable correlation in how one can connect with God's infinite power. Be certain that I learned that we have no power without *believing* in Him. The power, the answered prayers, the healing comes from Him and only Him, and once we *believe* and understand how to connect with Him, then the secret is revealed.

You see, I researched and began to *believe*, and once I tuned out the world and turned to Him, the Lord proved His word to be true as pointed out in Matthew 7:8 (AKJV):

> *"for everyone that asketh receiveth; and he that seeketh findeth; and to him that knocketh it shall be opened."*

I found that the thoughts you have every night are very important as you enter the alpha, theta, and delta brain-frequency levels, because this creates an energized connection with Divine energy, our ultimate Healer, God.

For the most part, if you have a lot of negativity and confusing thoughts in your mind, it prevents you from truly communicating your desire to Our Heavenly Father. It is as if your thoughts live in murky waters and are not capable of clearly expressing your true intentions. So making every effort to provide clear thinking as you pray and mediate is my best recommendation to you. This is the true secret of prayer, in my personal opinion, based on my research and experience.

Once I was able to change the recordings in my subconscious mind through prayer and meditation, my life literally began to change. I finally realized that I had God's number all along. In fact, we all do. It's just that the message I was giving Him in the past was all wrong. My mind was just too busy with negative racing thoughts, consequently causing the waters in my mind to be extensively cloudy. Once I learned to clear my thoughts and change them to positive thoughts was when my communication became comprehensible. That is why I say it isn't "what" we ask for, it is "how" we ask for it. I *believe* that this is how prayers are answered.

I find that too many times, people simply pray the words during a conscious state of mind, but they do not meditate on it, and they think negatively during the rest of the day. These negative thoughts then begin to replay in people's minds before they fall asleep.

Many individuals also hold a lot of resistance to this concept; therefore, their unfortunate circumstances persist. As another famous quote articulates:

*"What you resist persists."*
—*Carl Jung, a Swiss psychiatrist.*

The bottom line is, I came to realize that after fourteen years of researching all of my diagnoses and trying so hard to get better, my subconscious mind began to change without me even knowing it. The words my subconscious began to repeat every night were, "How do I control my mind versus it controlling me? How do I control my mind versus it controlling me?"

This actually became my new passion to figure out and was the most prominent question I had before going to sleep. Eventually, God heard my question's vibration without difficulty and He began to rearrange the Universe to offer me what He promised through scripture He would do. As a result, He began to guide me toward all of the tools I needed to figure it out.

I can only fathom that because I could not understand the first message of hope God brought to all of us when He sent His own Son, Jesus, into our lives, He decided to allow my son to bring me a message in a terminology that I could understand. I remain eternally grateful for His miraculous way of communicating with me through my own flesh and blood.

I really hope that this makes sense, because I am speaking from my own personal experience, based on what my research and my own reasoning told me was possible. I put *The Secret* to the test. I tried it, and by golly, it actually worked, and it continues to work every time.

If you are reading this book, then it must have happened again, because I am focusing right now on my desire to write a book that can help others escape from a confining life like the one I once had, and from the imprisoned mental anguish that took my father's life.

As I enter my creative and imaginary brain-wave frequency levels before I go to sleep, I envision other's engrossed with reading my testimony. I see and hear my family, friends, and people I don't even know congratulating me on what a great testimony God has honored me to give. The feeling I experience during this journey engulfs my body with feelings of pure elation. If I can help just one person as a result of this voyage, then my life's painful expedition was well worth it.

It is my *belief* that this is my purpose; this is what God wants me to do. I carried my cross for a reason, just as Jesus carried His and just as you too have your own cross to bear. Someone out there needs to hear my story, and perhaps that person is you.

The truth is that you really don't need to know how it all works, just know that it certainly does work. God gave you creative imagination, so why not use it? All you have to do is *believe* with unwavering faith and know, without a shadow of a doubt, it to be true.

Remember, whether or not this is still hard to understand, just try to comprehend that there is a greater energy that exists within you. That is where He is! Once you tap into it, it is completely life changing. You can even refer to the Bible, 1 Corinthians 6:19-20 (AKJV), where it quotes:

> *"...know ye not that your body is the temple of the Holy Ghost which is in you..."*

Actually, I found another biblical scripture that says we are all basically one with God. For example, 1 Corinthians 6:17 (AKJV) expresses:

> *"But he that is joined unto the Lord is one spirit."*

God's purpose was for us to live in an abundance of peace and love. It is our negative thinking that attracts all of the negative things in our lives. It is our doubt and lack of faith in *believing* that everything is possible that prevents us from recognizing our own

Godly potential. Our pessimistic nature keeps us from being at peace with whom we really are, one with the Spirit of God.

It is also written in Matthew 17:20 (AKJV):

> *"And Jesus said unto them, Because of your unbelief: for verily I say unto you, If ye have faith as a grain of mustard seed, ye shall say unto this mountain, Remove hence to yonder place; and it shall remove; and nothing shall be impossible unto you."*

The truth is that what I desire may not be exactly what you desire. What makes sense to me may not be exactly what makes sense to you, and what I am willing to do may not be what you are willing to do. Yet if you truly *believe*, where the end result connects you with this miraculous energy that lives within you—then you will witness for yourself how the Universe rearranges itself and how your prayers will begin to materialize! Just try it and allow the Lord to show you the way!

Again, I encourage you to read everything that you can and do your own research. However, you can read all you want until the end of time; you can gain all of the knowledge in the world, but it is only by putting your faith, *belief* and imagination into practice on a daily basis that, as time passes, you will see the results.

It's a way of life; you must become habitual in your practices. It's just like working out. You can have all of the exercise videos and equipment you want, you can have as many gym memberships as you want, but if you don't get up off the couch and work at it on a regular basis, you will never see the results that you want.

So, if you have ever asked yourself, "Where is He?" I am here to confirm that He lives within us all.

Regardless whether you agree with any of this or not, the best thing I can keep asking you is, "Do you have a desire to change? If so, how bad do you want it? How bad is your desire to change?"

# Chapter 9:
# A Spirit Saved

*"**Acquire** the **Spirit** of **Peace**
and a **thousand** souls
**around you will be saved.**"*
~ *Seraphim of Sarov*

AFTER UNDERSTANDING THE WHOLE God and Universe concept, this next occurrence was a definitive blessing for me. With all I had learned up to this point, and with the new relationship I felt I had developed with God, I never really expected the next level that I reached with Him. Once I got to know my Heavenly Father better through prayer and meditation, our relationship began to flourish into something more beautiful than I could ever have envisioned. Not only did I gain a closer relationship with Him, but I also developed a relationship with His Son. I was already impressed with Him, but what happened next just took my breath away.

During my tenure at school, I was living at my mother's house in one of her extra bedrooms. One Sunday morning, I took a break from studying and went channel surfing. I had periodically tried to watch some of those church channels they always broadcast on TV, but never found much fulfillment in the messages until this one particular Sunday.

As I clicked repeatedly on the remote control, I came across one church channel with a handsome young smiling pastor. For whatever reason, he caught my attention, and I stopped to listen to him. It seemed that everything he was saying brought my thoughts to, "Yeah, that's right. Oh, wow, that is so true. Incredible! That sounds similar to the hope expressed in *The Secret*!" So I kept listening and I watched the entire thirty minutes. I felt amazing afterwards. I found out that the pastor's name was Joel Osteen.

I realized that he was on TV every Sunday at 10 a.m., so each week after that I tuned in. Whenever I listened to him, I felt pure bliss. I could relate to everything he said. It was as if I wasn't alone anymore, in the way I processed my thoughts and reasoned about life. In my mind, I had finally found my church. How amazing that I didn't have to leave my house to attend! Yet sometimes, I wished his church would move to my home town, so that I could attend the live services.

Whenever my mom wanted to ask me something, if I was watching Pastor Joel I told her, "Mom, I'm at church right now. I'll come see you in a few minutes." It got to a point where she knew not to disturb me at 10 a.m. every Sunday morning.

Then, after a while, I realized that another pastor named Troy Gramling had a service that came on next. This Pastor caught my attention too, so I began to watch him as well. At this point, my church service extended from one-half hour to one hour every Sunday morning.

I always wondered why I'd never found a church like these back in the day when I was searching so much. Their message of hope was so breathtaking. Something about these two pastors captivated me and lured me in. Because they used normal day-to-day life experiences in their sermons, I could relate to them, and I was hooked.

I wanted to know what religion they practiced. The way they spoke was like nothing I had ever heard in any other church. I later learned that they belonged to nondenominational Christian congregations that solely studied the Word of God from the Bible. I found it fascinating, especially because I kept hearing the same message of hope that was expressed in *The Secret*.

I heard that Pastor Joel was coming to my area for what they called "A Night of Hope." I stayed tuned in, just waiting to hear the date. In mid-2010, the date was finally announced for Pastor Joel's upcoming arrival in December 2010. I immediately purchased my ticket, and when the day came, I went alone. I parked my car at the Metrorail station and took this train to avoid the heavy traffic and parking problems that I knew would be inevitable at such an event.

I cannot begin to put into words what an amazing service it was that I experienced. I was also pleasantly surprised when a little old lady sitting next to me told me how much she loved Pastor Joel, even though she was Jewish. This confirmed to me that Pastor Joel and his way of spreading hope and the Word of God touched everyone, from all walks of life. The entire place had such positive energy vibrating throughout that you could literally feel it flowing through your body. I felt illuminated with joy.

At the convention, I went "Joel happy" and immediately purchased a T-shirt. I went to the bathroom and put it on with pride. I also decided to buy a Bible and a Bible carrying case with the words printed on it that Joel says at the beginning of each service: *"This is my Bible. I am what it says I am. I have what it says I have. I can do what it says I can do. Today, I will be taught the word of God. I boldly confess: My mind is alert, my heart is receptive, I will never be the same. . . . In Jesus' Name."*

I fell in love with that carrying case, because I had memorized that saying by then. So I made my purchase, put my Bible in the carrying case, and went to the service. When it was all over, I left with the most incredible feeling of overwhelming inspiration.

Despite purchasing the Bible, I really never opened it, but I did put it next to my bed with the Jesus cross I always kept with me, and those two items alone gave me comfort.

Life went on: I graduated from college, got registered, went on vacation, got a job, and finally found a new apartment. One day the most bizarre thing happened. While on Facebook, I read a post from my son's cousin (a young man whom I call my nephew) that said he had just gone to church, and they had handed out free Joel Osteen books called, *Every Day Is a Friday*. I asked him about the church. Long story short, I found out that it was only five minutes away from my new apartment, and it was the church of Pastor Troy, the other pastor I had been watching on TV right after Pastor Joel each Sunday.

I was so excited! I couldn't wait until the following Sunday to go check it out myself. It may not have been Pastor Joel's church, but it was Pastor Troy's church, and that was good enough for me. I even remember seeing Pastor Troy at the "Night of Hope" event with Pastor Joel. That was all very cool, in my book!

When I got to church, the police were directing traffic outside to help the crowds safely reach their destination. There were people from all walks of life, and I was greeted by the friendliest cheerful people as I walked into the church doors. Even though I don't drink coffee, they were serving free coffee in the lobby, with lids on the cups so that guests could take the coffee in to the service. I had never seen that kind of thoughtfulness at any church before. This place was like no other church I had ever attended. There were three big screens on the walls and TV cameras with cameramen and a large stage. On the screens were inspirational messages, and beautiful music played on the overhead speakers.

When the service was about to begin, the band came onstage with their singers. The lights went off, the strobe lights came on, the people all stood up, and the worship began. I felt as if I were in a spiritual rock concert. It was awesome, because I love, love, love music. What a great way to praise God! This was all new to me, because they never showed this part on TV. It was a pleasant surprise. Then the live service hosted by Pastor Troy was incredibly uplifting.

After this, I could not wait for Sundays to come around so that I could attend again and again. This was my highlight of every week. Of course, I still watched Joel Osteen at 10 a.m. and attended Pastor Troy's church at 12:45 p.m.

This church is called Potential Church. Its motto is *"Bringing people together to reach their God's potential."* Wow, this made so much sense to me, because I had gradually been learning through *The Secret* that we all have God potential.

I started attending church in November 2011 and found out that they would be baptizing people at the beach on Christmas Eve. I wanted to learn more about baptism, so that I could take my spirituality to the next level. I had an unbelievable natural feeling inside, prompting me to take this new journey.

I started to ask a few questions about baptism, and I truly enjoyed what I learned. I was ready to accept Jesus Christ as my Lord and Savior, but Christmas Eve had been pre-planned with my family, my kids were coming into town, and I couldn't change my plans so suddenly. I just could not make it to the Beach Baptism that time.

The New Year came, 2012, and I continued to go to church alone. I really enjoyed the fact that it had no set rituals; you could go dressed as you were, and there were no judgments about anyone or any other religion. I felt really good there, and it beat staying home alone and watching it on TV.

Then I learned about their "fellowship groups," when a church member approached me and told me about groups for single members. I was told that we weren't meant to go through life alone. These groups consisted of single followers who meet up regularly for Bible studies and to go to dinners, movies, and events together. I decided to sign up and attend.

I remember feeling a little out of place during the first meeting because I didn't know anyone, but they all made me feel very welcome. They also held Bible study sessions. Most of them knew scriptures, and they said that for any questions we had, the answers could be found in the Bible. However, I had never been able to understand the Bible, so I felt lost.

Regardless, I did enjoy the conversations and the teachings. People spoke about their struggles and how the Word brought them the answers. When I mentioned that I didn't understand the Bible when I'd once tried reading it, they told me where to find Bibles that were written in easy-to-understand terminology.

A few days later, I woke up one morning and looked at my night table, realizing I still had the Bible I had purchased when I went to see Pastor Joel. Something told me to open it, and I discovered that it was an easy-reading Bible. I seemed to understand it perfectly. Thus, I decided to start by reading the New Testament, which is the story of Jesus.

I called the church and asked about their future baptisms and found out that they were baptizing that following weekend at the church. But I wanted to get baptized in my favorite place on earth: the beach, so I inquired about their next Beach Baptism. I was told that it would be done on Easter morning, but they hadn't announced it just yet. When the announcement happened, I could sign up then. So I patiently waited and signed up immediately after registration was open.

By that time, I had made a lot of great new single friends and had gone to the movies, to dinners, and even bowling. It was such a nice change of pace to have pleasant like-minded people to do things with. I even became friends with them on their exclusive Facebook page. Thankfully, I didn't feel so alone in my spiritual journey anymore.

Once I signed up for the Beach Baptism, I shared the news with my new friends to see if anyone wanted to join me. A few friends said that they had already been baptized the prior year, but they would come along anyway to cheer me on. I then learned of a few other friends who had already signed up as well.

In retrospect, it was a sad time, too, because when I told my family that I was going to be baptized, they really didn't understand it or my sudden fascination with the church. None of them had ever been interested in knowing God as much as I always had as a young girl. My mom even said to me, "But you were already baptized," and my brother also questioned me as to why I was doing it. As much as I wanted them to be thrilled for me and wanted them to be there, they showed no interest, so I didn't push the issue or hold it against them.

Nonetheless, my family always supported me in anything I wanted to do. All they ever desired for me was to see me healthy and happy, and I genuinely was. If that was good enough for them, then it was good enough for me, too.

I also wanted my children to attend, but they lived far away and were busy with their jobs and school, so they couldn't attend, either. Yet I felt so blessed that my new friends were willing to come and cheer me on. This was going to be a very special day.

The most exciting thing was that the baptism would happen at the crack of dawn, on the morning that Christians celebrate Jesus rising from the dead. It became so symbolic for me. I *believed* that this was the day I would finally put all of the turmoil of my old life behind me. I would be cleansed of all of the bad that had happened in my past. I would have a second chance at life.

So, I had made the decision to accept Jesus Christ as my Lord and Savior—not because people told me that was what I needed to do, but because it resonated strongly in my heart and soul. It was a deep vibrating desire that lived within me to do.

I *believed* in God, and I *believed* that He brought His Son to earth to wash away our sins. After all I had been through along this new journey I had embarked on, and with all of the miracles that

God had shown me, there was no doubt in my mind that this was the path I needed to take.

As a result, before my baptism, I felt that if I was going to take this journey, it was time I read the entire story of Christ, so that I could know Him better.

I have to admit that I read the Bible every morning before going to work. Most of the time, I didn't want to put the book down, I became so engrossed in it. It was such an easy-reading Bible that it was the additional spiritual food I needed and longed for during this time in my life.

The most interesting part of this entire journey for me was that the more I read the Bible, the more I could correlate its scriptures with the concepts *The Secret* had instilled in me.

This confirmed that the spiritual *belief* system I had acquired up to that point, which I discovered without knowing the Word of God, had actually been derived from the Word of God. Everything that had made sense to me, everything I had come to *believe* in, was all conveyed in the Bible. I was so mesmerized by it, because more pieces of the puzzle were harmoniously joining together in my life. I was convinced that throughout this entire journey, as I began to connect with that higher than life energy that lived within me, I was literally being guided by the Spirit of the Most High God. It was a journey to the light that I had always longed for.

I can remember the first time I read the Book of Matthew. I read a story that made me cry, confirming that I was right where I needed to be in life. This particular story was revolutionary for me. It was about a lady who needed healing really badly. When she heard that Jesus was going around healing people, she immediately went to see Him.

This story I refer to comes from Matthew 9:20-22 (AKJV) that says:

*"And, behold, a woman, which was diseased with an issue of blood twelve years, came behind him, and touched the hem of his garment: for she said within herself, If I may but touch his garment, I shall be whole. But Jesus turned him about, and when he saw her, he said, Daughter, be of good comfort; thy faith hath made thee whole. And the woman was made whole from that hour."*

Recounting this story brings tears to my eyes. You see, my story was so similar. I *believed* with all of my heart that if only I could tap into that higher-than-life spiritual energy, then I would be healed. My mind was in pure agony, in pure turmoil, in pure confusion, which threw me into intense therapy for fourteen years. I felt as if my mind had been bleeding for most of my life. Not until I turned and looked inward and began to have unwavering faith in this higher entity was I, too, healed.

So when I read what Jesus said to the woman, *"...Daughter, be of good comfort; thy faith hath made thee whole..."* was as if I heard Jesus say those words directly to me, too.

I continued to read and was able to finish the entire New Testament shortly before my baptism. I was so excited to accept Jesus as my Lord and Savior that the night before my baptism, I could barely sleep due to pure excitement. I felt like a little kid who was ready to go to Disney World.

That next morning I received a text message from my church, somewhat like a wake-up call, congratulating me on my new journey and saying that they looked forward to seeing me at the Beach Baptism.

I jumped out of bed and hurried to get my bathing suit on, grabbed my towel, and headed out to the beach at 5:00 a.m. When

I neared the beach and turned the corner to go to the section where the baptism would be held, I saw volunteers with smiling faces lined up by the curbside, wearing their light blue Beach Baptism T-shirts and waving us in. It was a very welcoming experience.

After I parked my car, I followed the signs that led us to the beach. There were people everywhere. I met up with my new friends, three of whom were going to get baptized too.

It was a chilly, windy morning and you could hear the waves crashing on the shore. I remember saying, "Oh, no, that water must be real cold, and I really don't like cold water." My friends and I chuckled with excitement.

It was pitch-black outside, but the full moon was shining, so brilliantly beautiful. Everyone lined up for his or her turn to go into the water to get baptized. The moment the daylight appeared on the horizon, people started to enter the water. I patiently but eagerly awaited my turn to go in.

As I waded into the water, it felt cool and refreshing—not a bit cold, as I'd thought it would be. Then the pastor prayed over me. After I was dunked and lifted out of the water, my spirit was literally reborn. The exuberant feeling that rushed through my body was beyond words. I hugged the pastor and all of the volunteers as I walked out of the water with my hands held up high, praising God for this amazing new life that He had offered me.

When I got out of the water, I hugged my new friends who had taken the time to wake up early to celebrate and greet me as I emerged from the water a new person. They even took my picture during my baptism when I surfaced, fully transformed. I then put on my light blue Beach Baptism T-shirt and went to breakfast with my friends. Thus began my journey in my new life.

After that, I decided to become a volunteer at church. I started greeting people, giving others the same joy I had felt when I first walked through those doors. It was my time to serve others.

The most unbelievable part of this particular journey was that this was the same beach I had gone to for the last twenty years when I was afflicted with grief, anxiety, and confusion. This beach had been such a safe haven for me that I always had a beach chair, a towel, and a gallon of water in the trunk of my car, because I never knew when I would need to jump in my car and escape from it all. So many times when I felt overwhelmed, I went to this beach alone in an attempt to clear my head.

Once, I even woke up in the back seat of my car, which I had parked at the beach during one of my dissociative moments. I didn't know how I got there, because I had no memory of anything, not even driving there. Apparently, even my subconscious mind fled to the beach when I experienced mental distress. It too felt at peace there.

This was also the exact same beach where I'd gone that one weekend to read the book *The Secret*. It was so ironic how much meaning that beach had for me. Yet, who could have predicted this would be the same beach that the Lord would choose for my Spirit to be reborn. When they say, "God works in mysterious ways," boy, they sure aren't kidding!

The baptism was the most beautiful, natural, and graceful event that I have ever experienced in my life.

This is why I *believe* in my heart and my soul, without a shadow of a doubt, that the God I longed for was the One Who brought me closer to Him and to His Son. When I read the entire New Testament, I found so many scriptures that directly correlated with the message portrayed in *The Secret*. I now *believe* that *The Secret* was designed to fulfill God's message in what many proclaim is a nontraditional path. God knew that some of His children have difficulty in understanding original scripture that sometimes causes so much confusion—confusion I experienced many times. *The Secret* and the easy reading bible published by

Joel Osteen actually speak to you in the same language as God intended you to understand, only in different terminology. Only God knows how to relay His message in different ways.

I want to express that I am not only a newly faith-based Christian, but more importantly, I am an amazing spiritual being. I am a child of God. I am Love, and Love is God. We are "One"! All I really want is to share with you a message of love and hope.

## Controversy Still Exists

I know that many of my fellow Christians may not agree that the way I found God through *The Secret* is the right way. However, I want to say one thing to my brothers and sisters in Christ. I didn't find God, He found me. I was one of His lost sheep, and He came out looking for me in the only way He knew I would understand. As the scripture poignantly reveals, in Matthew 18:12-13 (AKJV):

> *"How think ye? if a man have an hundred sheep, and one of them be gone astray, doth he not leave the ninety and nine, and goeth into the mountains, and seeketh that which is gone astray? And if so be that he find it, verily I say unto you, he rejoiceth more of that sheep, than of the ninety and nine which went not astray."*

Despite all the scriptures I quote in my book that I am able to relate with, I have found that many Christians still debate scripture as it has been written.

Even though I am not a bible expert, nor do I profess to be and have not studied it in great depth, I have done further research by hearing different Christian's points of view, and by doing so with an open-mind. I found that, for the most part, there are many different interpretations and perceptions about what has been written. I learned throughout the centuries the bible has been rewritten many times, consequently, bringing forth many different versions.

Some Christians proclaim that their interpretation and perception is the correct one. Some Christians call religion a cult and some live in tremendous fear, claiming that the Devil is the cause of so many Christian deceptions.

I even learned that in 1611, the bible that was originally written in another language was interpreted by a group of many people that eventually concurred in its English translation which is mostly accepted as the Authorized King James Version (AKJV), which is the version I mostly chose to quote in my book.

However, when I really try to make sense of it all, I attempt to understand the controversy that exists by many in reference to the accuracy of the bible's many translations. I witness these debates all the time which brought me to ponder about it all by asking myself, "Were the first words written back in the day precisely relayed?"

So, with that question in mind, could it be possible that somewhere along the year's, inaccurate information was not only relayed, but also misinterpreted in translation just as some declare is done today? Who is to know for sure if nobody that actually lived in those days can attest to the actual scriptures that were written, as they are not alive today to confirm that their version neither were correctly written nor translated? Neither can we go back to read the original writing for ourselves because we just cannot read the writings from their cultures language. I have even read that the original scriptures don't even exist anymore, although I cannot be sure that information is true either. So, what does one *believe*?

I guess this is where trust, *belief* and faith come into play.

I do my best to reason all of these disagreements by analyzing reasonable correlations. For example, I think about how students in college approach learning when listening to a lecture. Some students take notes and others may use a tape recorder. Isn't it possible that those that had the tape recorders would have a much better account of what actually was said, versus the ones that took notes?

How about the ones that just sat there and listened and didn't take notes or used a tape recorder, what then? You later bring all of them together and surely there will be many debating their different perceptions and interpretations of what was actually said in the classroom lecture, right? I would suppose that the ones with the tape recorder could prove they were correct by replaying the exact words spoken during the lecture. Despite the differences in accounts and regardless of who was most accurate, the overall message was understood by all having enough information to interpret it effectively enough to pass the final exam.

Well, back in the day, there were no tape recorders and surely they didn't have a pen and paper on hand to immediately write down what was said to the perfection of each Word that was spoken. Regardless, there is enough information written in scripture to correlate with each other that have lead us all to *believe* the story is true, but to what accuracy? Well, nobody will ever really know for sure because we weren't there. So, my personal reasoning determines that there are enough minor discrepancies in the different bible translated versions to debate regarding each word's 100 percent accuracy. However, there is also enough information for us Christians to *believe* in its purpose—to give us hope that something bigger lives within us that desperately wants to have a personal relationship with us all.

Putting all of this into perspective, I guess that was why when I was younger, every church I visited *believed* in something slightly diverse, which confused me so much. This has given me more proof of how people are able to interpret and perceive the Word so differently and some debate it so intensely. However, we hope that at the end of time, we will all pass the test.

Although certain skepticism in reference still exists in my mind regarding it all, overall I truly *believe* in the story of Christ. I am not one to profess which translation is right or wrong, but I do understand why so many people have so many debates. I found they all have substantial information where all sides have legitimate arguments in reference.

Many Christians even debate whether it is okay to celebrate the birth of Christ on Christmas or not—whether Easter really is the correct time to celebrate the death and resurrection of Christ, due to those days being of Pagan origin. I am sure that these debates will live on until the end of time, as I am certain that my story will, one day, become a big debate for many and will be criticized deeply by some.

Many have already verbalized to me that the messages I receive from my Higher Source and/or Divinity (GOD) are from the Devil attempting to make me *believe* something that isn't true. They cannot fathom why my life has panned out so beautifully opposed to theirs, even though they pronounce they are the true followers. They wonder why their lives aren't as glorious as mine. It's their *belief*, as they proclaim, because the Devil is deceiving me. They cannot grasp the notion that I am blessed by God nor that a Christian like me doesn't consider myself religious, but only as an energized Christian spiritual being as I *believe* God also is.

So, trust me, I am aware that some Christians, and even non-believers for that matter, are ready to spew out their disagreements and hateful comments towards my testimony. All I can say is that it is their personal right to *believe* and say whatever it is they want. I will hold no judgment against them, nor will I argue with them. I will continue on my path, holding dear the relationship I have with God.

I can only pronounce that fear, hatred and negativity will only produce more of it in their lives, and this I am convinced of. I pray that their hearts heal from such venom, as I only wish that their lives become as glorious as mine has become. My life may not be perfect, as it will never be, but it has become glorious and merciful without a doubt.

With that said: I am not here to debate with anyone because my story is only based on my life and my personal experience, and I am not here to rebut anyone's *belief* on the matter, nor that of their own personal experiences. The parts of the bible I quote that resonate so deeply within me are because of the direct correlation it has with my own personal life experience, which has proved to me that those words are true.

I choose to *believe* a supernatural energy exists—an energy that lives within us all that brings to us our own personal revelations.

How do we get these revelations?

My *belief* is by learning to stay quiet long enough to listen for the answers. It is my conviction that God will, without a shadow of doubt, bring the non-believers to *believe*. He will bring the confused out of confusion. He will heal those that have held unwavering Faith in Him. He will reveal to us the true words that were written. Therefore, it has been revealed to me that the scriptures I quote do originate from God and I *believe* in them with every cell that vibrates in my human flesh and in my energized spirit.

My friends, I would like to stress that I am not trying to change your point of view regarding God or interfere with your *belief* system. Neither is it my intention to imply that this is the path that you, too, have to take. It is simply the path I *believe* was chosen for me by God.

It is my *belief* that God has a path for you, too. It might not be the same path He had for me, because you are unique in your own way, so God has a unique path for you. You simply need to *believe* this is true.

If you think that reading my book right now is just a coincidence, think again. God knows that you have a desire to find your way and heal those wounds that are preventing you from reaching your highest potential, because He is the One Who placed the desire within me to write this book.

Sometimes I have no clue where the words I write come from, because although my experiences are real and truthful, it is my *belief* that the dialogue is all His.

As my life unfolded, I became even more grateful that I learned how to relax and lower my internal brain-wave frequencies. As I project positive thoughts, I stay quiet long enough for my energy's vibration to unite as One with that of our Heavenly Father's energy.

Finally, my friends, many of us will always wonder why so many who say they are God-driven have so many judgments against those who do not *believe* exactly as they do.

I hold dear to this next bible scripture:

> *"Judge not, and ye shall not be judged: condemn*
> *not, and ye shall not be condemned: forgive, and*
> *ye shall be forgiven." Luke 6:37 (AKJV)*

Not only do I witness Christians placing judgment on one another, but I also witness the government place judgment on others, which is so unfortunate. We are all sinners, so don't judge others just because they sin differently than you do.

Never forget what the scripture says in John 8:7 (AKJV):

*"...when they continued asking Him, He lifted up himself, and said unto them, he that is without sin among you, let him first cast a stone at her."*

I only pray that many can find their true higher selves and follow what they feel is best for them. Be happy with who you are and try to project only positivity and love out to the world. The truth is: we cannot force anyone to *believe* in something or live a life that they are not ready for. The more you try to change how others live, the less you will be able to change the way you do.

My best advice for you is to try to live as an example and show others what a great life you lead as a result. You might be surprised by how many people want the same blessings you have. You will ultimately observe how naturally their change comes about. Remember, you can only change one person, and that person is "you"!

I have no doubt in my mind that God will place before you the people and the tools you need to find the right path that is best suited for you, should you choose to continue on your own personal path of discovery. Yet, even though He may put all of the tools in front of you, because the Lord has also given us "free will" to do as we please, everyone can choose any path that he or she wishes. Looking for outward pleasures will bring you only temporary happiness. It isn't until you look deep within you that permanent happiness will materialize.

I was looking for a permanent fix and so was able to let go of things that produced only a temporary one. I am not perfect, as I continue to admit that I never will be perfect. Yet I have chosen to proceed along my spiritual path and I will keep working on my shortcomings, because I still have many.

I once read a saying that expresses exactly how I feel:

*"I am not a Christian because I am perfect; I am a Christian because I need a Savior."*

And Matthew 19:26 proclaims:

*"But Jesus beheld them, and said unto them, With men this is impossible; but with God all things are possible."*

As soon as I demonstrated unwavering faith, God not only healed my mind, but He also saved my spirit. He led me out of my confining mind and took me on a journey to the light.

I hope you enjoyed my testimony about how I *believe* God brought me closer to Him and to His Son.

Regardless of your own *belief*, the biggest question is for you to determine what it is that you really desire. Which path are you willing to take to get there, and, most importantly, you must be very clear about this: "How bad do you want it? How bad do you desire change?"

# Chapter 10:
# Miracles in the Making

*"I am realistic – I expect miracles."*
*~ Wayne W. Dyer*

WHAT I WANT TO SHARE now with you are a few testimonies on miracles that manifested in my life other than my mental healing. Once you truly get it, miracles will start popping-up in your life too.

## Coincidence or Manifestation?
## You be the Judge!

IN JANUARY 2009, I had just started going to college. This was the year my daughter would be of legal age, and both child support checks, from the government and her father, would stop. Because the housing market was so stagnant, I hadn't been selling any houses, either, so I couldn't depend on that supplemental income. As a result, I became concerned with how I could afford to continue paying my mortgage.

I also had to be realistic about the fact that going back to college would not allow me time to work at any job. Stress was my downfall, and now that I was better, I couldn't risk my health by stressing myself out with full-time school nor with any type of work. I finally realized that there was no way I could afford to live in my home any longer. So, I had no choice but to put my house up for sale.

Having real estate expertise, I became quite worried, because, due to the disastrous housing market crash, my house was worth far less than I owed on it. What a dilemma! I knew that the only solution was to ask permission from the bank to sell my house for its market value at the time. I owed approximately $159K, and the market value of my home had decreased to about $79K. Since I couldn't pay my mortgage any longer, I had no choice but to default and get approval from the bank to accept what I could get for the house and to forgive me the balance. In real estate terms, this was called a "short sale."

I hired a short sale specialist, because I wasn't too knowledgeable about how to handle a deal like that. It was a fairly new type of transaction that I had never done before. I did know, however, that a home in short sale status usually takes a long time to close, perhaps a minimum of ninety days simply to get an approval from the bank and approximately seven months or more to even find a buyer and close on the deal.

All I really wanted at this point was to be able to live in my house at least until my daughter graduated from high school at the end of May. Knowing the short sale process, I didn't think that this would be a problem, because I would probably live there longer than that.

I put the house up for sale at the beginning of February 2009. I immediately submitted my short sale request to the bank, along with all of my distressed financial information.

Since I had just started college and had already gotten off all of my medications, I decided to meditate on manifesting something new. I began to hope that I could sell my home to another single mom like me. I was so attached to my home after living there for thirteen years. I desired someone else to benefit from raising her kids in it as I was blessed to do. I had done so much work on it, and, knowing that it needed a lot more work, my yearning desire for someone to love and nurture the house was my goal. So I started praying to God and emerged myself in meditating on this.

Every night I visualized selling my home to a single mom. I also began to visualize myself moving when my daughter graduated at the end of May. To repel any negativity, I habitually practiced the saying, "I'm sorry, please forgive me, thank You, I love You."

I remember that during the entire month of February, there were no showings whatsoever. Not one person came to see the house. Then, in the beginning of March, I had three showings, back to back. The first showing was a single man, but he didn't make an offer. The next day a single mom with a twelve-year-old daughter came to see the house. The moment she left, I prayed hard that she liked the house enough to submit an offer.

Coincidentally: that same evening, I was informed by my realtor that the single mom had made a full-price offer. I was so happy, but the next day another buyer came to see my house. This buyer was an investor who put in a cash offer, and it was a little bit higher than the asking price.

Based on the little I knew back then about short sales, it was my understanding that all offers must be submitted to the bank for approval, so logic told me that the investor would win the bid.

I will never forget that evening after the realtor received the cash offer, as I lay in bed; I closed my eyes and started talking to God. I said, "Oh, my Lord, I am so sorry; please forgive me; thank You, I love You. I know that whatever is meant to be has to be, but I really want the single mom to live here. I'm sure she needs this house much more than the investor does."

I then put on my earphones and started to listen to my meditation/manifestation audio. I visualized the lady and her daughter happily moving into my home. I became so thrilled with it all. I needed to *believe* in my heart that the same God Who heard my plea about my medical healing would hear my plea now. I never told a soul about this, either.

Although I knew it was a long shot, I kept my faith alive. I remember the next morning waking up feeling profoundly inspired to call my realtor and express how I felt about both buyers. My realtor said that as soon as he heard back from the bank, he would let me know. I also knew that it was to the Realtor's benefit to acquire the higher priced offer, because his commission would consequently be higher as well. Either way, I patiently waited. I knew it could take up to ninety days before the bank responded and much longer to close, so I continued to meditate and visualize. What did I have to lose?

By mid-April, I got a call from my realtor with the verdict. The bank had approved the short sale, and the buyer would be the single mom with the daughter.

"Are you serious?" I asked.

"Yes," the realtor said. "Congratulations!"

He told me that the closing was set for mid-May.

I blurted out, "Do you think we can close at the end of the month instead? My daughter doesn't graduate until then, and her prom—what about her prom? I scheduled a limousine to pick up her and her friends at the house after that closing date. I really want to see if we can extend the closing, please."

My realtor said, "Let me see what I can do."

I have to tell you the truth, I prayed even harder then. A couple of days later, the realtor called me back and said that the bank would charge a penalty for every single day we extended the closing, and I would have to pay it. Of course, I couldn't afford to do this.

However, the realtor then said that he had spoken to the buyer, and she had agreed to close on the assigned date, and she would allow my daughter and me to live in the house completely rent free until the 30th.

I was speechless. I genuinely began to cry tears of joy. I felt ecstatic and eagerly said, "Tell her thank you. Thank you very much!"

As a licensed realtor myself, I just couldn't understand how this had happened. Normally, the buyer would ask for some sort of rent, at least, because as of the day of closing, it is legally the buyer's house, not the seller's any longer. The fact that she trusted me with her house and wasn't going to charge me a penny was simply unheard of. It was truly a miracle.

Immediately after hanging up the phone, I fell to my knees and thanked God for answering my prayers.

So, bottom line, I eventually sold the house to a single mom, I was able to live in the house until my daughter graduated from high school, and I could have the limo pick up my daughter and her friends in front of the home she had grown up in. It all happened just as I had imagined it, as I had envisioned . . . exactly the way I had meditated on it and prayed to God. I was flabbergasted.

Was this a coincidence, or was it a manifestation? I *believe* it was a manifestation, because otherwise it couldn't have worked out exactly the way I had envisioned it and had meditated on it, and as I had continuously prayed to God.

The only Entity Who is perfect is God, so I was convinced that the only way this could have turned out so perfectly was through His Divine intervention.

## The Biggest "Aha" Moment

THIS NEXT TESTIMONY was what truly confirmed to me that all that was happening in my new life were miracles God had placed before me. It was literally the biggest "Aha" moment I ever had to date. This manifestation was completely unexpected and so deeply profound. It solidified how the possibilities were endless, and how amazing the powers of prayer really are.

To give you a little background, in 2008, when I began meditating every night for a medical healing, and before I even fathomed that I would be going back to school and selling my house in 2009, what I really wanted was to remodel my home. Despite how much work I had done on the house, it still needed a lot more—so much so, that I once wished that the people from the *Extreme Home Makeover* show would come to remodel my home. I know that was a silly idea, but I really wanted Ty Pennington and his crew to visit me.

Since I was unsure how I would accomplish this remodeling, I decided to periodically do an extra mediation about how I wanted my home to look. Despite my efforts, I sold my home and thought that remodeling it just wasn't meant to be. Yet a few years later, in 2011, my biggest "Aha" moment resulted upon moving into my own apartment after having had lived with my mom during my years in college. Below is my journal entry the day this occurred.

**\*\*\*\*\*\*\*\*\*\***

## October 16, 2011

It is 5:30 a.m., and I got up with enough energy to put more stuff away in my new apartment. Now I am on my porch, enjoying the serenity. I guess I can begin by saying that "I am living in a little place in Heaven."

What does that mean to me? Well, let me ask you something. If there was some place on Earth that would make you feel as if you were living in a little place in Heaven, where would that be? Go ahead, ask yourself—be honest. If the perfect sanctuary existed somewhere, what would it look like? Close your eyes and envision it. How does living there make you feel?

I think I have come full circle with my manifestations. It's almost too eerie to think about, let alone live it, but it's a good kind of eerie. You see, yesterday I moved into my own apartment. It is the first time in my almost fifty years of life that I've ever lived alone. Alone, meaning no parents, no men, and no kids. Alone, with no help from anybody. I did this alone!

As I looked around my apartment, while organizing and putting my possessions away, some interesting thoughts came to mind about things I had wanted and envisioned in the last few years. For the most part, envisioning whatever I wanted in my mind gave me the exuberant feeling of already having it, and I was grateful to have lived through it, if only in my mind. If everything I'd imagined came together just the way I wanted it, then that would be my little place in Heaven.

Looking back now, I moved with my kids to a little three-bedroom, one-bath home after my second divorce. It was small, about 980 square feet. I bought it on foreclosure in November 1996 and had to do a lot of remodeling. My son was fourteen years old at the time and my daughter, four years old. I had initially put new white Formica cabinets in my kitchen. The appliances were white as well. It was a small kitchen.

I remember washing dishes, and to my right (facing me) was the stove. It was an L-shaped kitchen. To the right of the stove was the refrigerator. The appliances were very close to one another, without much countertop space.

Unfortunately, twelve years after I moved to this house, in 2008, the kitchen cabinets were looking rather worn out, and some of the hinges on the doors were falling off. No matter how hard I tried to screw them back in, the doors kept coming off the hinges.

During this time, my girlfriend had just remodeled her kitchen with the nicest cherry wood cabinets, and her countertop finish was so gorgeous, it looked like marble. Once I saw her new kitchen, I also wanted to remodel my kitchen cabinets and wished mine could look just like hers.

I remember that I used to sit on my loveseat in the living room and envision how I wanted my kitchen to look. Periodically, that is what I imagined during my meditation.

I sat with my headphones, listening to my meditation audio, as it guided me through an amazing spiritual journey. I imagined knocking down part of a kitchen wall that led to the living room. This would make it an open floor plan. There would be a counter overlooking the living room, where I could put a couple of stools. The openness would give this area the illusion that it was much bigger than it was.

"If only there was just a little more room in the kitchen, so that I could separate the appliances to give me more counter space," I pondered.

I even went to Home Depot to see whether this was a project I wanted to take on myself.

"Hell, I am pretty handy," I confidently told myself. But when I realized it was a much bigger task than I could physically do alone, I brought in some contractors to give estimates on refinishing the cabinets I already had. The price was too steep, so I continued to dream.

Consequently, I sold my home. My son was in the U.S. Coast Guard, and my daughter was off to college, and now it was my turn. It was time for me to move on. Yet even though I never got to remodel my kitchen and see my vision come to life, I didn't lose hope. Even while living with my mother when I attended college, I still dreamed of having my own pretty place one day.

More time passed, and less than a year after I moved out of my home, my brother bought a two-bedroom condo that I helped him purchase. He, too, had those nice wood cabinets in the kitchen and stainless steel appliances.

"Wow, I would love to have stainless steel appliances and a dishwasher. I haven't had a dishwasher for twenty years," I thought with excitement.

My brother also put in hardwood floors. "That looks so nice," I ruminated. "I'd love wooden floors, too."

So I envisioned having a pretty kitchen and allowed myself to feel as if I were cooking in that kitchen. I remember visualizing this many times. It felt so nice. I still had my faith, I still held on to my dream, and I still had hope. I continued to *believe* that this was possible one day.

I even remember, during the time I lived in my home, I had a very good friend who lived close by in a house on the lake. During some very stressful times, I went to his house to sit and look at the lake for hours and relax. He had a really nice *big* tree by the lake. It gave the right amount of shade on hot sunny days. I always told him it was the perfect tree.

When you were little, do you remember ever drawing a picture of an apple tree with a thick trunk, and it branched out perfectly? I personally remember drawing that kind of tree many times. Well, it was a tree just like that but without the apples. That tree was so pretty. My friend even had a swing hanging from the tree where I would sit and meditate. I felt total serenity sitting there.

As I sat there quietly, I drifted off in thought. "Wow, this would be awesome to have every day. Just walk to your backyard and be in total serenity. I would love this, too."

My friend had also remodeled his kitchen with wooden cabinets and marble countertops, and he put down wood floors, too. So I kept dreaming and envisioning, as I sat on the swing under that tree and stared at the lake. Hope was still alive in my mind. I might not have physically owned those things, but I would go to live in that place in my mind and always felt grateful for the experience.

Meditation is awesome!

Now comes the interesting part. Yesterday I moved into my new apartment, as I mentioned earlier. The porch off my living room faces a lake. I can not only walk out onto my porch every day and have that lake view, I can sit on my couch and turn my head, look out my glass sliding door, and there it is: total serenity. I also have cherry wood cabinets with appliances that look like stainless steel, and the floors have simulated-wood linoleum. I also have a dishwasher.

The eerie thing I noticed this morning, as I stepped back and took it all in, was that my new kitchen has the same exact L-shaped layout as my previous home's kitchen. The only difference is that the stove is on my left, not on my right. There is more space between the appliances, allowing more countertop area, just as I had envisioned in my home. The kitchen also has an open floor plan, with no wall separating the kitchen and the living room, and I have a counter where I could put a couple of stools.

Another peculiar thing I realized is that my cabinets are almost exactly the same as my girlfriend's cabinets—the ones I had envisioned that would look awesome in my home. I had just been to her house last night, and this morning I made the correlation. They have the same color and almost the same grooves on the doors, along with the same type of faux marble countertop, only a different color scheme.

I just now became conscious of the fact that I didn't have to be in the same home to see my vision come to life. All I needed was the vision, an imagination. I even have an amazing *big* tree in my backyard. It is situated between my porch and the lake. It has that perfect apple tree look, and the breeze blowing through its branches mesmerizes me, as I sit here and write.

I can honestly say that after I noticed all of this, it was an absolute "Aha" moment. This realization felt like an intense out-of-body spiritual connection.

Let me take a good look at this again. I got the kitchen cabinets I envisioned, appliances with the appearance of stainless steel, a dishwasher, floors that resembled hardwood, an open floor plan, and a counter for my stools. I got the lake and even got the tree, and my kitchen is exactly how I envisioned it, except that it is reversed: the appliances are now on my left, ironically on the side of my heart where I *believe* the Lord resides within me.

How can everything I envisioned from so many different places for so many years all of a sudden be all together in one place that is affordable to me? Poof... here it is!

Can you now better understand why I feel as if I'm living in a little place in Heaven? I may not have gotten it when I wanted it, but I got it when I was ready. I may not have gotten top-of-the line stuff, but it looks just as I had envisioned it.

I never lost my dream, I never lost my passion, I never lost my vision, and I never lost hope, because when you really want something bad enough, when you *believe* with all your heart and you can truly connect with your Higher Spirit (and, for me, His name is GOD), you can have whatever you want.

As the Bible quote in Matthew 7:7 says:

> *"Ask, and it shall be given to you* [I asked it was given to me]; *seek, and ye shall find* [I sought and I found]; *knock, and it shall be opened unto you* [I knocked and the door was opened].

After my medical healing and the selling of my home manifested, this was certainly the icing on the cake. My vision was finally brought to life in the most bizarre way, at the most unexpected moment.

I'll never forget how my mom kept expressing her fear that I would get sick again, as she watched me study so hard, while I kept myself confined in that one bedroom in her house. She had witnessed how strenuous that time was for me and was afraid that I'd have a mental meltdown again. She just could not fathom seeing me healthy for a long period of time, because she knew that stress had been a big trigger for me in the past. She could not imagine me ever living alone, either.

I did my best to appease her mind and told her, "Mom, don't worry, I feel fine. I'm going to be okay. This is just a temporary situation. One day I will have a great job and have my own place again. I am never going to get sick again. God has healed me. I know that God has something special waiting for me, Mom. I can see it. God has it all planned out for me. I trust Him mom, don't worry."

My mom may not have been able to envision my doing well, because her experience with me in the past was quite intense, so she allowed her fear get in the way. But that didn't matter, because I wasn't afraid anymore.

Every time she expressed any type of negativity, I closed my eyes and recited, "I'm sorry, please forgive me, thank You, I love You."

I *believed* that this would repel any negativity that she was generating in my direction. I held on tight to my vision, to my imagination, and most of all I held on tight to my faith. I *believed* that I had enough faith for both of us.

I could see my future in my mind's eye. It was engraved in my heart, and I became very grateful to God for giving it all to me, even before I ever had it. I cherished every meditation. I was grateful for that vision he had blessed me with. So I did the best I could to reassure my mom that everything would be just fine.

This goes to show how powerful unwavering faith in God is—the power of imagination, and the power of the "Law of Attraction"!

I *believe* that when you really live your life with a heart of gratitude for everything you have now, and you continue to dream and envision with your whole heart and soul where you want to be, it will come to pass—maybe not when you want it, but it will come to pass when God feels you are ready. You just have to **believe**!

It works the same way if you think negatively, and you are consumed with negativity. You will get what you think about, what you are passionate about, because what you envision makes you so heated about the situation that you live through it in your mind, even if it hasn't happened yet. All that you are creating is more of the same.

Trust me when I say: I know, because I lived like that for forty-six years of my life. This is why I conditioned myself to think the opposite of the way I did before, and it worked. I let my mind be consumed with positivity and faith in God. I had a dream, I had a vision, I *believed*, and I achieved. My life has changed forever.

Learn to look at the glass as half-full versus half-empty; for every negative, there is a positive. Just find the positive, and focus on that.

As I said, this experience for me was the icing on the cake. This had to be written down and shared one day, because it really is an incredible story. I know, without a shadow of a doubt, that I will continue to experience more miracles in my future.

I once thought I was *alone*, but I really wasn't, because I had God by my side every step of the way. His were the footprints in the sand that I saw. He was the One Who carried me to this apartment, where He allowed my vision to come to life. It was like being blindfolded for so many years, and, suddenly, the blindfolds were removed. Surprise!

********

## More Insight to Manifesting:

Aside from these two manifestations, so many more materialized in my life. For example, I also manifested my first job after graduating from college that allowed me to get my little place in heaven. It may have taken me five months to get my first job, but the way God rearranged the Universe was also amazing. Then after 15 months working, I hit a bump in the road. I was laid-off, but in less than one month I was offered another job. This time I actually manifested my dream job in a hospital working with the most amazing team of individuals I had ever worked with in my life.

Unfortunately, I had to relocate for my new dream job, leaving my little place in heaven behind and moved into an apartment that wasn't anything near what I once had. The hardest thing to leave behind was my lake view. But, I never lost hope, because I *believed* that arrangement would be temporary. It isn't so much what happens to you, it is how you handle what happens to you. So, I was now grateful for my dream job while accepting my, not so perfect, new apartment.

Nonetheless, after a year when my new lease expired, guess what? I was able to manifest another little place in heaven that was even better than the first. The best part was that I had my lake view back.

With that said, the many manifestations that have occurred in the interim have all been magnificent as well. All these manifestations had a few things in common; I used the same concept to manifest them all: mediate, imagine, visualize, ask, *believe* and feel the feeling of receiving it. At all times, I remained with an attitude of gratitude.

I am sure that it can all pan-out for you, too, if only you don't give-up in finding your way. You must also *believe* that you too can attain it all.

In my next chapters I want to stress a few more things that are crucial in manifesting. Although I have briefly disclosed certain steps, it is important that you really understand all the things I did that work hand-in-hand with the daily prayer and meditation practices I have already shared with you. Nobody ever taught me how to do all of this, so I would like to give you more insight into how I implemented all of what I learned into my daily life.

There is no doubt that my way isn't the only way, but I can only share with you everything else I did that worked for me in conjunction with what I have already shared thus far.

As you grow into your own awakening process, you will find the things that are best suited for you. At the least, what else I am about to share with you is a start to get you going towards the miracles of manifesting those things you truly desire.

So, before you move on to the next chapter, I would like to give you an assignment. I encourage you to get out a piece of paper and write down everything you want. I mean everything. There are no limits to getting whatever it is that you wish for. Be specific, and they have to be things you want really badly. If all you want is to be happy, then what is it specifically that will make you happy?

One important point I want to make that you should always remember: If what you want doesn't manifest exactly how you wish; know in your heart it is because, most probably, God has something better for you than what you wish for yourself. Sometimes we wish for something that isn't for our best interest, and you must *believe* in your heart that God knows what is best for you. Just stay in Faith, because He *will* bring you something better. So don't go against the grain.

Another important tip I can give you is that material things will never bring permanent happiness, because the day those things no longer exist, your happiness too will vanish. So if it is only happiness you are looking for, searching within is the first place to start. Ask the Lord to bring you internal peace first and to guide you to your purpose on this earth.

For example, if you feel that finding the perfect mate is the only thing that will bring you happiness; I can assure you that you will never be able to find true happiness next to anyone if you yourself have not attained true happiness on your own, within your own soul. Once you reach that point, requesting another soul to enter your life with like-minded attributes is the next step.

I can attest that this is possible, because after being alone for eight years, it wasn't until I found true happiness within myself that God unexpectedly brought into my life a very special man with like-minded attributes. It is possible folks! So, don't lose hope.

Try to master the art of meditating first, if nothing else. This can take some time, but don't give-up. It is important that you learn how to quite your mind long enough to recognize that internal intuitive thought that you will be receiving. It is like a thought you never had before, but a thought that suddenly makes a lot of sense.  It is a thought that penetrates so deeply within you that helps you recognize it as something beyond your own personal thought process.

Nonetheless, for now, it is important to write down everything you want, regardless of what it is. Just go with me on this exercise. If nothing else, it will help you take a step back and know yourself a little better.

Then I want you to diligently go through your list and pick out one thing that in your mind and in your soul resonates so deeply that you *"believe"* it is realistically attainable to you at this time in your life. Then, rearrange your list and put that particular thing on the top of your list.

Remember, we all want a lot of things, but it is that of which we *"desire"* deeply that we should focus on. Do you desire healing? Then ask for that. Do you desire a job? Then ask for that. Then make sure that your answer is "really badly" to my question, "How bad do you want it? How bad do you desire change?"

# Chapter 11:
# Important Ingredients

*"The greatest discovery of all time
is that a person can change
his future by merely
changing his attitude."*
*~ Oprah Winfrey*

I HOPE YOU WERE ABLE to take some time to make a list of all of the things you want. I also hope that you went through your list to figure out the one thing that you desire the most really badly. If you did, then by the end of this chapter, you will be one step closer to putting *The Secret* to the test, as I first did in 2008.

I make no guarantees that everything will work out perfectly for you, because I cannot control how badly you desire something or the real effort and faith you possess. Nor can I control how deeply you *believe* in it all. However, I want you to take the opportunity to give it a shot, just as I did. If I could do it, I see no reason why anyone with the same amount of determination, assertiveness, thoroughness, consistency, *belief* and faith cannot achieve the same results. I also have a very special treat for you at the end of this chapter, so stay with me, okay?

After reading *The Secret*, my entire attitude changed. Although everything I read and saw in the movie affected me deeply, some points were more prominent than others.

I don't know what your particular situation is; perhaps you have already read the book and/or watched the movie *The Secret*, and nothing has worked out for you as you had hoped. Maybe you've never even heard about *The Secret*, much like my own psychiatrist had never heard of it either. You may have even lost confidence that anything could actually work for you. It really doesn't matter if it hasn't panned out for you yet. The important thing to know is that every day is a new day to start doing what you never did before. Allow your attitude to change and allow hope, *belief* and faith to live freely in your heart.

This is why I asked you to make your list. My goal is to help you turn things around and experience miracles, as you have always dreamed of doing. It is a process of clearly knowing your purpose by first changing how you think about your life.

I truly appreciate a quote by Christian D. Larsen, who lived from 1866 to 1954 that once said:

> *"That a man can change himself . . . and master his own destiny is the conclusion of every mind who is wide-awake to the power of right thought."*

In *The Secret*, I learned that once you are able to go to your happy place through meditation, the first important ingredient is to "ask". In life, if you want a medical healing, you ask for it; if you want a job, you ask for it; if you want something specific, you ask for it. Just ask and keep asking! Whatever your deepest desire is, just ask for it.

However, asking alone isn't enough. The second concept is that you must "*believe*" that what you have asked for has already been given! You first "ask" and then you "*believe*"! I cannot stress enough how important it is, during meditation, to "*believe*" that you already have whatever you want. You do not *believe* that you *will* have it, not that you are *going* to have it; but instead, you *believe* that you "already" have it. Unwavering *belief* is crucial. (*Belief* means *accepting that a declaration is true or that something exists, without having any proof.*)

When you can meditate with this much *belief*, you generate an amazing positive spiritual vibration.

Let me give you an illustration of the concept of *believing* in something. Do you remember during your birthday or a particular occasion when you were asked by your parents what it was that you wanted, and you *"believed"* that once you expressed what you wanted, you would get it, for certain? Even if you didn't experience this, just go with me on this one, okay? Well, that is the same kind of *belief* you must have when you ask God for what you want. Know without a shadow of a doubt that God is going to give you whatever you ask for. That is the same concept; it truly is that simple.

The third concept is to "receive." You first "ask," then you *"believe,"* and then you "receive." Now go back to the previous story again. You know when you received that present you desired so much, that you *believed* you were going to get, and that feeling of pure joy when you saw it? Well, that is the same thing you do when you meditate. Allow yourself to receive it and put yourself right there, feeling how having what you wanted makes you light up inside. Envision having it and holding it, enjoying the feeling as you cherish and embrace it. Allow yourself to take pleasure in that excitement. The "feeling" of already having "received" it is such a key ingredient to prayer and meditation.

The fourth step that is just as indispensable is "gratitude." You must allow yourself to feel gratitude for having received it. For example, when your parents gave you something you really wanted, didn't you hug them and shower them with love and gratitude? Well, this concept is no different. You must show gratitude to God (the Universe) for giving you exactly what you wanted. You must do it with pure love, joy, and sincere gratitude. You must go through the emotions as if this was real, because for that moment, even if only in your mind, it is real!

Then you must let it go and trust that what you have asked for has already been given. You must *believe* that it will all come to pass.

It is important not to put a time frame on getting what you want, because doing so will only disappoint you. You see, God (The Universe) doesn't work on your time frame, but only when the time is right. Yet if you start to lose faith in getting what you want, you lose the positive vibration you sent out to Him.

When you stop *believing* and stop having faith, in a way, you are basically saying that you will never have it. So, in the back of your mind, you change your energized vibrations, and the Universe picks up on that vibration too. You will manifest whatever you *believe*. If you *believe* you will "never" have it, then you "never" will have it.

You see, the Universe grants you your every wish, because it doesn't matter if you say you can or you can't, the Universe will always prove you right! So if you say you can, then you will, and if you say you can't, then you won't. It really is common sense, don't you think?

During the beginning stages of my psychotherapy, I used to say, "But I just can't make these bad feelings go away!" One of my therapists once said to me, "If you say you can't, you won't!" I got so angry, because I didn't feel that this therapist understood me; didn't understand my pain or my struggles. The truth is that I didn't understand what she was telling me back then, because no one had ever explained it to me, but now I get it. That is why I am making every effort to help you get it too.

Before I move on to explain more powerful tools that you can use, I want to clearly communicate that if you do not feel comfortable with anything I suggest in this book, you should not follow along if you don't want to, okay?

Also, if you are under the treatment of a medical professional, I highly recommend you consult with them first before you undergo any changes to your current treatment plan.

Remember, I am only sharing with you everything I did and how I did it in hopes that it will, somehow, be beneficial to you. However, I don't recommend you to follow through with it until you consult with your medical professional first.

Please take note that I am just sharing with you what worked for me, but you must understand that I am not a licensed therapist nor medical professional, so do not take my sole advice as the final verdict to your personal journey in life.

Nevertheless, should you feel ready to proceed, first and foremost, I encourage you to watch the movie *The Secret*. It doesn't matter if you have already watched it before; I urge you to watch it once again! Try to keep your mind and heart open.

I know for a fact that if you have a Netflix account, you can watch *The Secret* online for free. Also, you can go to *The Secret*'s website at **http://thesecret.tv/** and watch it for a small fee, or you can buy the movie on *The Secret*'s website, on Amazon.com, or at a local book store, such as Barnes and Noble. Recently, I found that you can even access the entire movie on YouTube. You can decide which route to take, but I recommend that you just watch it! I have no connection to *The Secret* and I don't benefit from you watching it in any way, shape, or form. The only beneficiary is you.

Also, I am offering you below the actual website to that 20 minute meditation/manifestation audio I keep talking about. It is a free download, and again, I do not benefit at all if you download it.

**www.mindpowernews.com/ManifestationMP3.htm**

All I can recommend is for you to listen to this audio with earphones. I always prefer doing this before going to sleep, because, it is obvious to me, this audio guides you as you consciously enter the alpha and theta levels, which reinforces the healing that occurs in the subconscious delta level.

Once I conditioned myself to do this before I went to sleep, I found that eventually I was able to consciously lower my brain-wave frequencies at any time of the day allowing myself to obtain the same results whenever I desired.

First, try to condition yourself to go to that happy place every night when there will be no interruptions; then you will find it easier to do it at any given point. If this audio is not working for you, just keep searching for one that will. I know now that Oprah and Deepak Chopra offer a 21 day meditation program that is very helpful. I have also tried the Silva Method Meditation techniques as well. Feel free to Google them. Do your research and listen to your comfort zone and listen to whatever feels right for you, and then use that.

The free audio website I shared with you was my favorite, because it really helped bring my imagination to life, and it allowed me to experience all those feelings I mentioned above that were very important in bringing about my manifestations.

When I went through this process myself, I knew I was planting seeds, and I wasn't going to let anyone "disturb my crop." You must know in your heart and soul that this crop you take care of every day will eventually produce a bountiful harvest.

Now, take the one thing you picked out from your list that you most desire and first watch *"The Secret"* movie, because it will give you so much more information than what I can offer you at this point. Then listen to the audio, go to sleep, and then come back and read the next chapter of this book when you are ready. I also encourage you to keep a journal of this journey you are about to embark on. If you keep up with it all by remaining consistent with this practice, one day you will be astounded by the results!

As I conclude this chapter, I want to leave you with a wonderful quote from Jeremiah 29:11-13 (NIV):

> *"For I know the plans I have for you," declares the LORD, "plans to prosper you and not to harm you, plans to give you hope and a future. Then you will call on me and come and pray to me, and I will listen to you. You will seek me and find me when you seek me with all your heart."*

So, it is time for me to remind you again to ask yourself these questions: "How bad do you want it? How bad do you desire change?"

# Chapter 12:
# Taking Action

*"I know that I have the ability to achieve the
object of my Definite Purpose in life, therefore,
I demand of myself persistent, continuous action
toward its attainment, and I here and now
promise to render such action."*
*~ Napoleon Hill*

HELLO AGAIN, MY FRIENDS! Did you take action? Did you do what I recommended? Did you watch *The Secret*? Did you listen to the audio before going to sleep?

It makes a lot of sense to me that some of you did and some of you did not. Some of you just want it more than others do, or perhaps some people are still a little skeptical and want to keep reading to see where this is all going. And if you are just waiting to consult with your medical professional, then I am very proud of how careful and responsible you are.

Whatever your reasoning, that is okay, because we are all in different places in our lives. Not all of us are ready to use the tools that are handed to us. Some things are not for everyone, and that is fine. I still *believe* in you and am confident that you will find your way in due time. For those who did as I encouraged, congratulations to you! You have just taken the first step toward manifesting.

Regardless of whether you did or did not do what I suggested, I urge everyone to continue reading as many books on the subject as you can. Keep searching for whatever catches your attention enough to motivate you to take action and/or continue your journey of enlightenment. I'm just handing you the tools that worked for me, out of the countless tools that are available out there.

Anyway, let's say that you went ahead and did what I recommended. You made your list; you picked out one thing from your list; you watched the movie and listened to the audio recording. If you did, then perhaps what I have been talking about now makes much more sense to you. That is great and dandy.

However, even though you took action once, you must clearly understand that you need to do it again and again and again. Trust me, you will come to a point where you won't need to watch the movie or listen to the audio anymore. There will come a time when everything will come naturally to you. You will be able to go to bed, quiet your mind, lower your brain-wave frequencies, connect with your higher energy, communicate your deepest desires, thank Him and sleep like a baby, just as I do now. And if you ever falter, you know how to pick up right where you left off.

Remember, this is about reconditioning how your mind works so that you can allow yourself to generate a positive energy flow, and everything you desire will subsequently start showing up in your life.

I want to give you an example: let's say that you want a new job, just as I did. Just because you meditated last night, it doesn't mean that you can sit back, put your feet up, and wait for that job to fall from the sky. You have to take action. You have to be diligent in looking for work and applying and keep visualizing the one job you really want to have. Envision yourself working at this new job, just as the manifesting audio walks you through the process.

If this is the first time you're doing something like this, just keep meditating on it. Remember, reconditioning the subconscious mind is extremely important, because, unfortunately, every time you watch the news, they are talking about how bad the economy is and how many people are out of work. It seems that as if everywhere you go, people are talking about how bad their lives are due to the bad economy. No matter how you look at it, these are negative vibrations that you are receiving. Somehow, this seeps deep into your subconscious mind. Once all of this settles within your soul, you begin to *"believe"* that no matter how much you look for a job, due to such a bad economy, you will never get that job you want. Hey, I can only talk from personal experience.

This is why I encourage you to tune out the media and all of the negativity from other people. They are probably the biggest source of mental poison in your life. Do your meditation before you go to bed every night, until you realize without a shadow of a doubt that you will get that job, no matter whether society says otherwise. This concept works with anything you picked from your list that you really want.

Let me tell you another little secret. It just so happens that I started my journey of using *The Secret* at the beginning of the worst economic recession in our generation, while I was also suffering from one of the worst mental illnesses known to man. In addition, people everywhere were losing their homes, going on unemployment, and going on welfare, and many were having major nervous breakdowns because of the overwhelming amount of stress they were experiencing. Some people even committed suicide. This is how bad the economy was back then, and it can still be considered pretty ruthless today. Life has been so horrible for most Americans, so much so that it truly breaks my heart.

Yet during this stressful and agonizing economic collapse, I personally have felt the healthiest I've ever been, while living in the best economic conditions I have ever experienced in my life! I went back to college and not only got one great job, but when I lost that one, I immediately got another that was even better than the first. I had to give-up my little place in heaven to only get a better one a year later. I live a very happy life; I have never been sick mentally or physically since my healing, and I got off disability benefits because I didn't need government assistance anymore. It was the complete opposite of what many other Americans experienced.

How could that happen when statistics proved that everyone else was doing so poorly? And you know what? It all turned around for me once I put the concepts in *The Secret* to the test. I remained in faith, and every day I habitually used all of these tools that I'm now handing to you. I'm just saying, "*Believe* it or not!" God rearranged the Universe and brought these powerful tools to me, yet I was also given free will to do with them as I pleased. Nobody twisted my arm and told me I had to use them. I could choose to use them or not. You have the same choice to make.

I know that I mentioned that gratitude is crucial during meditation, but I have to admit that gratitude is important in everything in your life. When you are able to feel gratitude for everything you already have, you are generating positive vibrations out to the Universe. I can assure you that the more gratitude you feel, the more things God will give you to be grateful for.

*The Secret* elaborates how effective gratitude is, so I urge you to take action and implement this into your daily life. I personally practice the suggestions in *The Secret*, for example, when I get out of bed every morning. The moment my feet hit the ground, I give my thanks to God for the gift of waking up another day, for allowing my legs to walk, for allowing my eyes to see, and for allowing my heart to beat. I give thanks for the bed I slept in and the roof over my head. I give thanks for my car, for my job, for the food I eat, and so on. I literally give thanks for everything in my life, every day, all day long. I habitually do this from the moment I wake up to the moment I go to bed. Throughout my day, my mind literally is saying, "Thank You" for everything. I have become extremely passionate about giving gratitude.

If you watched *The Secret* movie, then you will better understand this from some of the anecdotes they discuss.

I remember that Lee Brower had a very good story about gratitude. When Lee was apparently having some family issues, and things just weren't going right for him, he decided to take a rock as a reminder to be grateful. He called it his "gratitude rock."

I even found interesting the words spoken by a man named Wallace Walters who lived from 1860 to 1911 who said:

> *"The daily practice of gratitude is one of the conduits by which your wealth will come to you."*

I still find it fascinating that all of these things I have mentioned thus far are not only powerful, but very simple to do. However, it is so difficult for people to actually take action and implement these concepts in their lives.

Never forget, you can know all of this and agree with it, but if you don't take action and incorporate it into your daily life, then it is utterly useless to you. It is more likely that you will revert back to your old conditioning, which hasn't given you all that you want yet. Taking action one day and not the next won't work. You must maintain the same kind of mind-set every single day.

I admit that I have faltered in the past. As much as I know what to do, I, too, fall down and scrape my knee, so don't get discouraged, and stay in faith. Nobody is perfect, so just stay determined and keep pushing forward. I *believe* in you!

The first step includes not only acknowledging that you want to change, but the fact that you must be clear about what you so badly desire to change. Second, you must figure out what you are willing to do to make that change. Third, once you have figured all of that out, you must be willing to take action and make it a habit to keep doing so.

I decided to learn how to ask, receive, and feel the feeling of already having it, and I became grateful for receiving it. I learned to have gratitude for everything in my life, and not only for what I envisioned in my meditations, but for everything during every moment of my life. I made a conscious commitment to do whatever was necessary to recondition my negative subconscious mind. I made the decision to do all of these things every single day. Even watching *The Secret* movie and listening to the audio every single night was a commitment that I made to myself. You see, I took action!

This is what made sense to me and what I *believed* would work for me. I wanted change in my life that badly. So, I encourage you to keep on reading and discover where your comfort zone is and what you are willing to do to make the change you badly desire. What commitment are you willing to make right now and every day thereafter?

And most important—you know where I am going with this, right? "How bad do you want it? How profound is your desire to change?"

# Chapter 13:

# Forgiveness

*"For if you forgive other people when they sin against you, your heavenly Father will also forgive you."*
*~ Matthew 6:14 (NIV)*

I BELIEVE THAT FORGIVENESS is an important aspect in productively moving forward with life. I have learned that practically everyone, from every walk of life, has someone who once did him or her wrong. Whether it is a family member, a friend, an ex-partner, a coworker, a stranger, or someone else; regardless of who this person is, someone once did something to you that caused bad feelings within you.

I'm sure that these feelings are so bad that every time you even think about whoever hurt or betrayed you, your insides begin to boil with anger, or you may feel hurt and pain. So, what do you do? You tend to stay away from this person and do your best not to think about him or her. If anyone even mentions this person, you may lash out with negative comments about the individual. I'm sure you can think of someone right now who falls in this category.

Unfortunately, these bad feelings are always with you, in some form or another, whether you like it or not. I know exactly what that feels like, because I have had my fair share of people who have done me so wrong, I cannot begin to mention all of them. As much as I wanted to forget all of the bad things they did to me, in my subconscious mind, those bad feelings persisted and manifested in behaviors that I sometimes could not explain. That is how powerful the subconscious mind is.

How many times have you gotten angry and yelled at someone just because he or she did something that reminded you of what someone in your past did to you? You were not really angry at the person you yelled at, but instead, you were angry at the person you were reminded of. Sometimes you don't even know why you lash out, but your subconscious mind does. Perhaps we all have these "mind drawers" where we store information that can escape when triggered. You don't have to suffer from a mental illness, as I did, to experience this. Have you ever said to someone, "I'm sorry, I don't know why I reacted that way"?

Through psychotherapy, I discovered the importance of forgiving and moving on. I knew that I had to learn to forgive, so I began by forgiving my father. I had so many horrible memories of him that I finally realized he was the main reason why I wanted to die at the tender age of thirteen.

I knew that I didn't have to forgive him because he deserved it; but that I had to forgive him because I deserved it. I didn't deserve to go through life harboring such negative feelings, stuck deep inside my soul. I spent so many years blaming him for my horrible life that I didn't know how to let it go. I may not have thought about each incident every day—in fact, for many years, I didn't even remember them—but my subconscious mind never forgot.

I started to practice forgiveness long before I learned about The Secret. I began to forgive my father about two years before his passing. He had gotten older and more passive in his ways. I remember finally forming a relationship with him. I was very grateful that my forensic psychiatrist helped me with this, because when I was forty-one, shortly before my father died, I finally became "Daddy's little girl," as I had secretly longed to be all of my life. That alone was a great healing for me.

Once my father passed away, I began to write in an attempt to figure myself out. It was kind of like putting together the pieces of the puzzle that made up my life. I decided to enhance my own personal self-discovery process in this manner. So much had surfaced in therapy over the years that writing it all down and putting the memories that surfaced into chronological order seemed like the only thing that made sense to me at the time. I hoped that I would be able to take a step back and see who, what, when, and why I was so messed up. I didn't expect to write a book about it; at the time, this writing was more of a personal task that I did for myself. I needed to know what had happened in my life that screwed up my mind. By the end of that journey, I realized how much I needed to forgive other people, yet I still found it extremely difficult.

Forgiving my dad was just a start. Regardless of my personal journey, I still experienced frequent bouts of depression, a lot of highs and lows, and my personalities wouldn't go away. I needed more help to take me to the next level of forgiveness.

Then, when my son gave me *The Secret* to read and I was finally able to open up to bigger and better ideas that made sense to me, I realized why forgiveness was so important.

In one section of *The Secret*, Lisa Nichols explains good feelings and bad feelings. She talks about bad feelings such as *"depression, anger, resentment, guilt."* Now these were feelings that I was all too familiar with. I felt anger and resentment toward all of the people who had previously hurt me. I also felt guilty that perhaps I had done something bad to provoke them to hurt me so badly. All I knew was that I didn't want to feel this way anymore. I was willing to do whatever it took to change all of that.

Lisa also describes the qualities of feeling good, such as, *"excitement, joy, gratitude, love."* These were feelings I wanted to have all of the time. Of course, at the beginning of learning this, I was still in the discovery stage. However, one thing was certain: I wanted to shift the way I felt all of the time. I ultimately realized that I needed to continue to forgive everyone who had ever hurt me, regardless of how difficult it was.

I mentally acknowledged that I felt bad because that was how others had conditioned me to feel. I had given them control over the way I felt. It was time that I took control of my life and reconditioned myself to feel good through forgiveness.

I also had to realize that these people who hurt me had probably been hurt pretty badly when they were growing up too, or perhaps their conditioning about what was right or wrong had inadvertently clouded their judgment. I had to somehow understand that they didn't hurt me because I did something wrong; they were simply acting out because of what someone had done to them or due to their lack of education about life in general. This was how I could accept that I needed to forgive all of them; just as I had forgiven my father. I'm not saying that they were right in what they did to me; it's just that I understood that they, too, were hurt in some way or simply didn't know any better, which was simply not their fault.

The reality of the situation is that we are all born as innocent children who grow up in an environment we have no control over. We are all conditioned based on what someone else has taught us. As a result of acknowledging this, I experienced an overwhelming feeling of empathy toward everyone who had hurt me.

Once I reached this point, I was able to fully forgive myself, too, because I could remove the guilt I felt. It was such a relief to realize that none of it was my own fault. This was a huge milestone for me.

Although forgiveness is very, very hard, I *believe* that once you figure out what you want in your future, you will realize that harboring bad feelings hurts only you, but does nothing to the perpetrator. The moment you decide to let go of all of those bad feelings, you will set yourself free to enjoy life as it was meant to be: abundant with love and good feelings.

So, it's important that you do your best to forgive and rid yourself of any bad feelings. You want to do everything possible to generate only positive vibrations toward the Universe. Harboring ill will toward anyone only produces negative vibrations, which in turn interfere with the positive path you are trying to stay on.

Don't let anyone rob you of what you want and deserve. Don't give anyone control over your life. Just allow people's karma to play out. In case you haven't realized it yet, everyone will sow what they reap, especially if these individuals never turn their lives around and seek a better path. Don't burden yourself with anything that is rightfully coming to someone else, except that which is rightfully due to you.

Remember to wish everyone well and share the love that lives deep within you. Continue generating positive vibrations and allow the Universe to take care of the rest.

As the saying goes, *"Leave it all in the hands of God!"* That is what I learned to do.

Once I was able to see life from that perspective, I could remove the darkness of everything that had been done to me, because my soul began to journey into the light. It has been a long voyage for me, but I can truly tell you that every day I now experience an abundance of *"excitement, joy, gratitude, and love."* I find myself smiling all the time. I love life as I have never loved it before. I love all people, regardless of their personal *beliefs.* I do my best not to judge anyone. I might not understand some people, but it is not for me to judge them or how they choose to live their lives.

I do my best not to impose my *beliefs* on anyone, although I do enjoy sharing my testimony with everyone. I stay away from people who insist on projecting negativity out to the world and those who do things that I may disagree with. However, I love everyone regardless.

We are all God's children, and it is unfortunate that most of us have been screwed up in one form or another. We all have issues, and we all have our own paths to travel on. I am just grateful that I learned how to fully forgive.

To forgive is to remove negative energy from your soul. To forgive is to rid yourself from the harm that others have done to you. To forgive is to set yourself free from your past. To forgive is to take control of your life. To forgive is to enable yourself to love and be loved.

Don't take the power of forgiveness for granted. If you really want change, I encourage you to dig deep into your heart and forgive everyone who has ever brought you pain. You don't have to hang out with them, you don't have to see them, and you certainly don't have to bring them back into your life, not if you don't want to. Forgiveness is a way of letting go of the bad feelings that have lingered within your soul for too long, as you now make room for the good feelings. Forgiveness is an internal feeling that brings you peace, love, and joy. Forgiveness is healing!

I want to close this chapter with a reminder of the absolutely horrific beating that Jesus received prior to His crucifixion and some of the last words He uttered as He painfully hung on the cross. In Luke 23:34 (AKJV), Jesus cried-out in agony,

*"Father, forgive them;*
*for they know not what they do..."*

If you want change in your life, I urge you to forgive. In life, you "live," you "learn," you "forgive," you "laugh," and then you are able to ultimately "love life." But first, you have to determine, "How bad do you want it? How bad do you desire change?"

# Chapter 14:
# Flip the Switch

*"The Person who sends out positive thoughts*
*activates the world around him positively*
*and draws back to himself positive results."*
~ *Norman Vincent Peale*

I WANT TO TALK about something called the "Flip Switch" method. I learned about it when I purchased an online audio program from Dr. Robert Anthony, who teaches a course called *"The Secret to Deliberate Creation."* You can look it up online if you'd like.

Dr. Anthony's course is similar to all of the "awakening" information that is available out there; everyone gives you something different to think about. You will relate to certain concepts from some of them, and you might think that others are a bit too much or get too complex in their explanations. It's up to you to listen to them and figure out what makes sense to you. The concept of flip-switching made a whole lot of sense to me when I first heard about it.

This all has to do with conditioning the conscious mind. You know—the mind that is thinking all the time while we are awake, the beta level? *The Secret* tells us that we have so many thoughts during the day, it is impossible to really monitor every thought. Even though we live in a remnant of our thoughts, we do have a time delay. Basically, if we catch ourselves when we have a negative thought, we have the ability to immediately hit the delete button and replace the negative thought with one that is positive. This prevents us from storing that negative thought in our subconscious "mind drawers."

Even though meditation is very important to program the subconscious mind, it is crucial that the conscious mind follows suit. Because, remember, the conscious mind is what I like to call "the subconscious programmer," so we need to keep the negative thoughts from getting programmed in the first place. If you are cleaning out your subconscious with meditation, it would be counterproductive to then reprogram it with new negative thoughts. So, when Dr. Robert Anthony described the flip-switch method, it really hit home.

I was able to relate this concept to *The Secret* as well, because Bob Proctor also speaks about changing a bad thought to a good one. It is the same idea, just with a different approach.

"Flip switch" is the ability to catch yourself at the exact moment you become aware of having a negative thought. It forces your awareness to acknowledge the negative thought and stop it dead in its tracks. This awareness allows you to flip the switch in your mind. Then you can change it to a positive thought.

Dr. Robert Anthony encourages you to find something in your past that made you very happy. Pick something so that when you think about it, the memory immediately gives you such happiness that it vibrates in every cell in your body, so much so that it makes you smile. It just automatically makes you feel good.

I found it intriguing how this concept also correlates with the meditation/manifestation audio I suggested that you listen to. The meditation audio helps you do this during meditation, during your alpha and theta levels. The flip-switch method helps you when you are not meditating, during your wide-awake beta level. Do you see how everything fits together?

It's funny how I began to understand the way to change my negative thoughts to positive ones from *The Secret*. Next, I found the meditation/manifestation audio from a completely different source, and then I learned the flip-switch method from someone else. This is why I encourage you to research, read, learn, and find what makes sense—then take action. All of these things combined enable a powerful energy shift to occur.

I decided to use the birth of my kids as my happiest thoughts during my unconscious and conscious mind reprogramming. I had such an amazing experience when they were born that every time I think about the first moment I saw them, I feel pure elation and joy running throughout my entire body.

Perhaps it wasn't so pleasant when your kids were born. I know a few women who didn't find it too enjoyable. Maybe you don't even have kids, so just choose the one thing that brings you a lot of joy and use that instead.

Now, every time you catch yourself having a negative thought or making a negative comment, immediately tell yourself, "Oops, that is a negative thought. I need to change that to a positive one." Then close your eyes and imagine the happy thought that you know will help you feel good, and hold that thought for about fifteen seconds. Allow yourself those fifteen seconds to simply "feel" happy. You'll be amazed at how that positive thought can override the negative one.

It is all about awareness, catching and flip-switching the negative thought to a positive one. The problem is that when people start to do this, they realize how many negative thoughts they have in a day, and they simply get tired of it and just stop. I guess they choose to keep the negative thoughts in their minds, and we all know what that means: they will consequently attract more negativity into their lives. It is just the "Law of Attraction" at work, folks!

I remember once when I was trying to explain to my son that he had to flip-switch his thoughts, he replied, "But Mom, that is so hard to do!"

I chuckled and modestly responded, "All the more reason you should do your best to keep doing it. If it is that hard, then you must be having a lot of negative thoughts during the day."

In one of my Bible study classes, I sat back and listened to the way some people were struggling with negative thoughts. So, I brought up the concept of the "Flip Switch," and I was amazed by how many people liked the idea. It really is common sense, but an idea that we really don't think much about. Then again, you can know about it, understand it, and agree with it, but if you don't "take action" and practice it every day, what use is it to you?

Again, it is all about developing awareness and the acceptance that you need to change. At the beginning, it might be difficult, but when you practice it more and more often, you will find yourself having to do it less and less, because you will start to recondition yourself to think positively more often than you think negatively. It really worked for me. Try it and you'll see!

It is important to align your conscious mind with your subconscious mind in order to receive the maximum amount of positive results. Once you "take action" and practice flip-switching, forgiveness, and the ability to quiet your mind; you learn how to ask, *believe*, receive, and express gratitude; and you engage in imagination and connect with your higher energy, you will experience miracles beyond your wildest dreams.

I know this sounds like a lot to do, but just remember, this stuff is very potent, because if it got all of those wacky personalities who lived deep within my subconscious to vanish and never come back, then it is without a doubt some very powerful stuff. Remember, the power already lives within you. All you have to do is gain access to it.

So, from now on, be aware of your negative thoughts and flip-switch them as many times as you have to. Eventually, you will find yourself doing it less and less often. Just do the best that you can. Now that you are aware of this technique to implement, you might start using it.

Take it one step at a time. Most people give up on *The Secret* because the truth is, you really have to make some serious daily changes in your life. So many changes that people sometimes just give up and say, *"The heck with all this, it is too much trouble."* Then they go on complaining about why *The Secret* doesn't work and why their lives are still so miserable. They proceed to blame everyone who has ever done them wrong for the horrible and miserable lives that they are living. They even blame the government for why life just plain-out sucks!

I lived like that for forty-six years. I know the feeling—been there, done that. My personal situation pushed me to want change really badly, and I was willing to do whatever it took to change my life around.

Isn't it time to start taking control of your life? Now is the time for you to know, without a shadow of doubt, "How bad do you want it? How bad do you desire change?"

# Chapter 15:
# Affirmations

*"Any thought that is passed on the subconscious*
*often enough and convincingly enough*
*is finally accepted."*
~ *Robert Collier*

WHAT ARE AFFIRMATIONS, you may wonder? When you affirm something, you acknowledge, confirm, and *"believe"* that something is real. If you tell yourself certain things over and over again, whether they are negative or positive, they will resonate so deeply within you that you will bring whatever you *believe* into your reality.

An example I want to share with you on how affirmations conditioned my subconscious mind while growing up is how I deeply harbored things that my dad used to tell me, over and over again. In Spanish, he would say, "Tu eres la mierda de la familia!" (You are the shit of the family.) He would further say, "Nunca seras como tus hermanos!" (You will never be like your brothers.)

My brothers never gave him any kind of trouble and always achieved better grades than I did. Both of my brothers also successfully graduated from high school and went to college, and we all know how my life turned out, right? I guess my father thought that by continuously telling me these disparaging things, I would somehow straighten up and strive to be more like them; however, the opposite became true in my life.

The repetition of his words made me *believe* they were all true. The pain this brought to my conscious mind pushed these affirming thoughts to my subconscious mind, and they stayed with me for a very long time afterwards. This also left me with an aching and bruised heart.

So, at some point, I stopped trying to be anything more than what my father taught me to *believe*. As a result, I began to live a life tainted by very low self-esteem, *believing* I would never be as successful as my brothers. Before I ever *believed* in God, my brothers were my gods; I idolized them. They were my heroes, and I *believed* that I wasn't worthy to ever measure up to such high standards.

This is just a brief description of what I mean about *"believing"* something is real. If you are told something often enough or tell yourself something often enough, you will eventually *believe* it to be real, even if it isn't. I may never have really been what my father claimed I was, but I surely *believed* it to be true; therefore, it consequently became my reality.

These were only a few of the negative thoughts that lingered for many years in my subconscious mind. I *believed* that I deserved all of the rotten things that happened to me. I just took life as it came and did my best to deal with it. I *believed* that I had no control over my life's outcome. I was destined to live in pain and agony.

During my new journey toward healing, it was time to change all of that. In the movie *The Secret*, they talk about vision boards. This is a positive affirmation technique that allows you to visualize and mentally repeat the things you desire in your life. Yet I learned and used many other techniques that I will share with you as well.

The way you use the vision boards that are discussed in *The Secret* is to cut out pictures from magazines of everything you want and post them up where you can see them every single day. You can hang these pictures on your bedroom wall or bathroom mirror or put them on your refrigerator. Seeing these pictures every morning when you wake up and every night before you go to sleep keeps the positive "feelings" prominent and alive during your conscious state.

The more you do to make yourself "feel" good, and the more you recognize how much you don't like to "feel" bad, reconditioning your overall behavior will, eventually, come naturally.

Another thing I learned was to write down positive statements. For example, if you want to feel good, write, "I feel great today." If you want a new car, write down, "I love my new car." If you want a new house, then write, "I love my new home." It is important to write in the present tense and not write something like "I want a new car/house" because you will find yourself always "wanting" it, versus actually "having" it. This is another reconditioning tool that works hand in hand with all of the other tips I've mentioned.

I also suggest writing down all of the things that you are grateful for. This is a very powerful exercise. Daily gratitude helps you experience much happier feelings as well.

I remember doing these exercises over and over again on a daily basis in the beginning, until I really didn't need to do them anymore, and all because it became natural for me to think about them during my entire day. Everything that I learned to do to think positively, I did without hesitation. Remember, it is all about properly conditioning yourself. That is how badly I desired change in my life. I took "action" every single day.

As I continued to research online, I stumbled upon something called "Mind Movies." I really got into this, and I think it is another extremely powerful tool to have in your repertoire. You can find examples on YouTube if you just type in the search box, Mind Movies. This is almost the same as the vision boards, but this time you bring the pictures to life through a picture slide show with instrumental music.

I first purchased a *"Mind Movie"* program that was for sale, and then I learned how to use the *Microsoft "Movie Maker"* program that you can download for free online. I ultimately made my own mind movies that way.

Basically, you go on the Internet and find images of all of the things that you want (for example, a car, a house, a job, and so on). Then you save them on your computer. You upload the pictures in either the *Mind Movie* or *Movie Maker* program or any other program you have. Simply line them up in a slide show. You then insert affirming statements to match each picture.

I found this technique shortly after my medical healing. Since I wanted to remain healthy, I found a picture of a healthy human cell and put these words on the clip, "Every cell in my body is healthy."

Now, let's say you want a particular car in a particular color. On the picture, you insert the words "I have the car of my dreams." Then let's say you want to attract money. Find a picture of money and insert the words "I am a money magnet." Let's say you want a particular type of home. You do the same with the picture, and you might insert, "I live in my dream home."

Once you have all of the pictures lined up with their powerful affirming quotes, add an instrumental audio track to accompany the slide show. Then sit back and watch that every night. This also helps you to concentrate and better envision these things when you meditate. I find this technique to be much more powerful than the vision boards, although I still like posting up pictures around my apartment, too. It keeps me focused all of the time.

Another thing I incorporated into my life during the one-hour drive to and from school was listening to positive music. I noticed that most of the songs I used to listen to contained sad lyrics, so I decided to make a CD of songs filled with positive, happy, and inspiring lyrics. I now only listen to music that inspires me and makes me smile.

The last thing I did when I moved into my new apartment was to purchase pictures with positive messages to hang on the walls. For example, I have a saying carved out of wood that reads, *"Live, Learn, Laugh, Love, Life."* Next to the door that overlooks my breathtaking lake view, another message says, *"Life is not measured by the amount of breaths we take, but by the moments that take our breath away."*

One of my classmates even gave me a beautiful plaque as a house-warming gift that recites, *"Life isn't about waiting for the storm to pass, it is about learning to dance in the rain."* Funny how she had no clue about my mysterious personal voyage, and how I seemed to attract this amazing gift into my life.

It doesn't matter where I go in my apartment, there are always positive messages that keep my thoughts on the right track.

You must be thinking how extreme I have taken all these techniques, but it's important to remember how deeply "imprisoned" my mind was in negativity. Seriously, who do you know who suffers or suffered from multiple personality disorder? I was surely in a place that flooded my mind with negative thoughts for most of my life. After being able to remove all of that negativity from my life, I have vowed never to allow my mind to revert back.

Even though I acknowledge that the world is full of negativity, at least while I'm in my home, in my own world, a world I have control over, I keep everything positive, bright, and cheerful.

There are some days when I get tired and frustrated, too, don't get me wrong. Yet now it doesn't matter where I look in my apartment, I can look up and see something positive. It truly helps me just to sit there and reflect on how important it is not to let day-to-day obstacles overwhelm me.

I have full control over my life now, and I will not allow other people's negative vibrations to overpower my mind ever again. Being in my world means being in a positive world, no matter where you go!

I have even developed a Facebook Fan page where my purpose is to share daily positive, inspiring and motivational messages with all of you. If you would like to receive these messages, just go to the website below and "like" my page. Hope to see you there as we journey to the light together.

https://www.facebook.com/journey2thelight?ref=hl

With that said, I don't expect everyone to take the extreme measures that I have chosen to incorporate into my life, but if any of the things I did or still do can help you in any way, then it is worth me sharing this information with you, regardless of how bizarre you may think it is.

Once you begin to think positively more times than you think negatively, you will begin to turn over a new leaf in your life.

There is one more very important thing that you should always keep in mind. Do you best to refrain from uttering the negative words "I don't" or "I can't." When you catch yourself thinking like that, you need to "switch" your thoughts to what you "do want" and to the things you "can do." Instead of saying, "I don't want to be late," switch it to "I am on time." Instead of saying, "I don't want to fail," say, "I am a success." Instead of saying, "I can't do that," say, "I can do anything I put my mind to!" The affirmation technique works really well to keep you from using the negative words "I don't" and "I can't".

You may not feel the need to incorporate all of these reinforcing affirmation techniques into your life, and that is okay. However, I have met a lot of people who are nowhere near as mentally messed up as I was, but they surely have some of the most negative attitudes I have ever seen. Certainly they could benefit by implementing some of these techniques in their lives. Simply decide which affirmation techniques you like best and then use those. Because remember, everything you decide to do is for your benefit and your benefit only. The path you take will be determined by the passion you have to bring change into your life.

In order to determine your passion, you must first know, without a shadow of a doubt, "How bad do you want it? How bad is your desire to change?"

# Chapter 16:
## Never Give Up on Your Dreams

*"The future belongs to those who believe in
the beauty of their dreams."*
*~ Eleanor Roosevelt*

MY FRIENDS, AS I CONCLUDE this book, I want to encourage you to never give up on your dreams. Once you determine how bad you want something, you'll realize that you have finally figured out what your dream is. Anyone can dream, but those who want their dreams badly enough are the ones who will convert their dreams into reality.

By this time, there have been many more dreams that have manifested in my life that are just as impressive as the few I mentioned: too many to mention in this book. So I am convinced, without a shadow of a doubt, that you too can accomplish every dream you desire.

Have you ever wondered what happens when we make New Year's resolutions? We all want to make a change, but it's usually something we think we need to do and not necessarily what burns as a deep desire within us. And why do we wait to do it on the New Year? Don't you think that if it's something you want to do really badly, you would be willing to do it at any given point in your life?

Well, we make that resolution in the New Year because that is what everyone else does. That is the trend. Then, in the same way that we make the resolution at the beginning of the year with everyone else, we give up on it right along with everyone else, too, so now we won't feel so bad. The first thing we do is make excuses why we don't stick with it. Hey, I've been there and done that, just like everyone else. The truth is that it wasn't something we wanted badly enough. It's that simple.

In addition, we are also conditioned to *believe* that we cannot have everything we want, that if God wanted us to have something, then He'd just automatically give it to us.

I remember my father once saying, "If there was a God, I wouldn't be going through such hell!"

Honestly, I was conditioned to think like that, too, for most of my life, until I discovered *The Secret*. It pains me that my father killed himself before learning what I know now.

I guess that is another reason I have such a burning desire to reach as many people as I can and give them my testimony. I may not have been able to save my father, but perhaps I can make a difference in someone else's life.

Now that I have a strong bond with God and have seen firsthand how changing the way I think, pray and meditate has completely transformed my life, I'm here to disagree with the notion that we get only that which God is willing to give us.

I *believe* that God is willing to give us all that we want; He is just waiting for us to ask Him the right way. You need to build a personal relationship with Him. Saying you *believe*, going to church, and then going about your life complaining, blaming, judging others, and filling your thoughts with negativity just won't work.

Yes, you will stumble across good things in your life, but for the most part, you will never really accomplish what the Lord wants you to accomplish, which is a life abundant with pure love and happiness. God may want good things for you, but if you don't "desire" them badly enough for yourself, if you don't *"believe"* that you are worthy of them, then you will keep living a life without the things you really long for.

You are obviously looking for answers or else you wouldn't have picked up my book, right? There is something inside you that wants to change, but you just don't know how—just as I didn't know how for forty-six long years of my life. You are not alone, my friends, you are not alone.

If one of your passions is to change; then, this book is meant to help you. If all of the things I chose to incorporate into my everyday life worked for me, then why wouldn't they work for you?

I know that right now there is a dream resonating within your soul, but it is simply clouded by a lot of man-made negativity that constantly surrounds us in this world. Perhaps you don't really know what is holding you back. There are probably things hidden so deeply in your subconscious that even you cannot tell what they are.

Simply change the way you think now—change your attitude. Do the exercises I described before you go to sleep, and do the exercises I recommended while you are awake. You really don't need to know which recordings stored in your "mind drawers" are holding you back; just know that you can change them to whatever you want them to be right now. You can start sending positive vibrations out to the Universe, where the Divine is waiting patiently to receive them.

I'll bet that after you read further into my latter chapters, you knew how I was going to end each one, right? You knew I would ask you, "How bad do you want it? How bad do you desire change?" I just wanted to prove to you how mind conditioning works. The more you read something repetitively, the more your mind is conditioned to think about it.

One of my hopes is that every time you start thinking of something that you want, you will automatically ask yourself, "How bad do I want this?" The moment you feel in every cell of your being that you want something so bad you can taste it, you will recognize that this is what you really desire; this is your true dream. Then you will do whatever it takes to fulfill that desire by "taking action" and making the daily "commitment" needed to obtain that dream that resonates so deeply in your soul.

I cannot help you or anyone change his or her life. I can share my experiences with you, and I can hand you the tools that worked for me, but it is up to you to use them. Each individual has to do that for him or herself. Some people are simply not ready for change; others just don't know what they really desire. I wrote this book in hopes that you can look deeply within yourselves and find your life's purpose. Then, and only then, will you find yourself committing to doing what you have to do in order to manifest everything you have longed for all your life; to live out your every dream.

I even try to teach all of these things to my kids. And do you think they listen to me all the time? No! Of course not. I try hard to reinforce it in them, but I realize that I cannot make them use these tools, either. As a parent, all I can do is remind them and try to set an example—an example I didn't know how to set when they were little.

I realize that my mental health has affected them a great deal. They both experienced depression that scared the hell out of me. They gained their own perspectives on what was actually happening to their mommy. They both rebelled; they both have found themselves with a negative mind-set; and many times they both felt beaten by life. I assure you that they still do at times. I am just so grateful that I was able to turn my life around when I did, because as I healed, they have also embarked on their own healing paths too.

My son is on a more consistent positive path right now, but I see certain things that he still tries hard to work at. The best part is that he is growing into his own skin and finding his own, unique way in a manner that suits him and his needs. It is a beautiful thing to see his spiritual growth, as he overflows with peace, love and happiness. The wisdom he possesses advances him way beyond his years. The determination that expanded within him after getting married and having his own son makes me Proud of him beyond words. The journey I see him entering now in entrepreneurship is one he has developed by "taking action". I know, without a shadow of doubt, that he, too, will reach his every goal and fulfill his every dream. I am grateful that he learned the concepts I teach to be invaluable in his new career.

My daughter, being nine years younger, is still experiencing various emotional roller-coaster rides. Yet I see an incredible spiritual shift occurring in her, as she not only acknowledges the miracles in my life, but is starting to experience miracles in her life, too. I am now seeing her spiritual soul blossoming into a burst of positive magnetic energy. She may still struggle with some things, but she is much further along than she once was. I am grateful to see that as many times as she falls down, she is learning to pick herself up, because she is also moving forward and becoming stronger. As she ventures out in her own new career in Performing Arts, I see her passion and creative abilities developing in ways that nobody else could have ever fathomed possible. I see her resilience in pursuing a career that many may have felt was a dead-end road, but by staying true to her own personal *"belief"* and "passion", she has made the "commitment" necessary to succeed at her personal goals and dreams. I am proud to witness her "taking action" and hurdling over every obstacle that has been set before her. This is the beginning of a journey to her fruitful success. I know that she, too, will attain every dream that she envisions for herself.

I am not going to sit here and profess that once you follow a more positive path or do all of the things you feel you should do, that you will never encounter negativity in your life. However, I can tell you with certainty that once you figure out what you want really badly, it does come a lot easier. You will learn how to prevent others from invading your positive world. Then again, if you just don't want a positive change in your life bad enough, nobody can make you change.

Another positive quote that I try to remember when unexpected events happen in my life is the Serenity Prayer:

> *"God give me the strength to accept the things I cannot change, the courage to change things I can, and the wisdom to know the difference."*

Once you are able to recondition how you think, it becomes much easier to think positively, and the negativity of this world will gradually affect you less and less. When you see how amazing all of this is, it will motivate you to keep at it.

At first, you will probably experience a lot of resistance, but when you fall, don't be so hard on yourself. Just remember that every day is a new day, so pick yourself up, brush yourself off, and then start again. The more you fall, the stronger you get. And remember, all you really have is NOW, so make the best of every NOW moment.

One important lesson I learned is that we all fail our way to success. The key is to never stop pushing forward towards your dreams no matter how many times you feel you have failed, because one day you will experience success just as you had imagined it, if not better. I can, confidently, sit here in saying that I have failed my way to success, and all because I never gave-up!

Simply figure out what you so badly want to change in your life. Figure out what your dream really is, and follow it. Don't let anyone ever tell you that you cannot accomplish what you want in life, because you can do whatever you set your mind to do. I *believe* in you, and so does God, so never lose hope and faith.

I hope my book inspired you. I hope my book gave you a lot of positive things to think about. You don't need to agree with everything I have said. You don't have to possess the same exact *belief* system, either, but my hope is that you gained enough out of my book to make the change that you are so desperately looking for in your life.

If nothing else, remember that it wasn't until I tuned out society's opinions, perspectives and interpretations on how life should be lived, tuned out all of the criticism, and tuned out all of the unnecessary man-made negativity in this world and started to look within myself that my mind was healed, and my spirit was saved. I was let out of that confined and dark world I desperately wanted to escape from—that secluded place where I lived in my mind. I was finally able to break-free from mental illness, and my journey to the light began.

As is stated in 1 John 4:4 (AKJV):

*"...greater is He that is in you,*
*than he that is in the world."*

So remember: Never, and I mean never, give up on your dreams.

With much love and gratitude,

*Jenny*

# References

The Book and Movie *"The Secret"* by Rhonda Byrne
The Book *"Zero Limits"* by Joe Vital
The Book *"Wishes Fulfilled"* by Wayne Dyer
The Book *"Hope for Today Bible"* by Joel Osteen
*The Secret of Deliberate Creation* by Dr. Robert Anthony
https://www.afsp.org/understanding-suicide/facts-and-figures
http://theovernight.donordrive.com/?fuseaction=cms.page&id=1034
http://www.toolsforwellness.com/brainstates.html
http://www.psychic101.com/brainwaves-beta-alpha-delta.html
http://en.wikipedia.org/wiki/Subconscious
http://www.abundance-and-happiness.com/super-conscious-mind.html
http://en.wikipedia.org/wiki/Beta_wave
http://www.ncbi.nlm.nih.gov/pubmed/12699709
http://www.iempowerself.com/71_law_of_belief_systems.html
http://www.merriam-webster.com/dictionary/self-discovery
http://www.mayoclinic.org/diseases-conditions/depression/basics/definition/con-20032977
http://en.wikipedia.org/wiki/Bipolar_disorder
http://www.webmd.com/mental-health/dissociative-identity-disorder-multiple-personality-disorder
http://healthymultiplicity.com/
http://www.mayoclinic.org/diseases-conditions/endometriosis/basics/definition/con-20013968
http://www.mayoclinic.org/diseases-conditions/premenstrual-syndrome/basics/definition/con-20020003
http://www.iempowerself.com/71_law_of_belief_systems.html
http://dictionary.reference.com/browse/exalted
http://www.merriam-webster.com/dictionary/heathen
http://www.thefreedictionary.com/unconverted
http://www.gotquestions.org/original-Bible.html

Printed in Great Britain
by Amazon.co.uk, Ltd.,
Marston Gate.